Spiritual Pedagogy

*A survey, critique and reconstruction
of contemporary spiritual education
in England and Wales*

Spiritual Pedagogy

*A survey, critique and reconstruction
of contemporary spiritual education
in England and Wales*

Andrew Wright

Culham College Institute

First published in 1998 by

Culham College Institute
The Malthouse
60 East St Helen Street
Abingdon
Oxon OX14 5EB

ISBN 0 907957 53 6

Contents

Foreword

The modest size of this book is out of proportion to its considerable importance. One of the highest duties of an academic researcher is to seek out and address those questions which are of most fundamental significance to contemporary society, and Andrew Wright's work on the spiritual development of our children certainly passes this test. He has illuminated the issues involved in the current debate on spirituality and has provided a valuable resource for those concerned with religious education at every level, not least in an ample bibliography.

The increasing concern over the past two decades about the spiritual development of pupils in our schools represents a welcome shift of emphasis from an undue preoccupation with the content of what is to be taught to a consideration of how the awareness of the learner might be deepened and enlarged.

The urgency of the debate has been fuelled by the reality of social fragmentation and the understandable determination on the part of those responsible for the education service not to be involved in a yob creation scheme.

The yearning for an understanding of spirituality wich would contribute to social cohesion has led to the establishment of a new orthodoxy in which it is suggested that access to a realm of universal spiritual experience can be achieved by primal intuitions unconstrained by any particular religious traditions. In this new orthodoxy, Christianity and Islam are represented as local and often limited editions of this universal spirituality. Mike Newby, writing as an expert in religious education from Kingston University, puts the matter very clearly:

> For reasons of tact and discretion, it is unwise to specify offending sub-traditions, as well as politically and socially harmful. It is important, however, if we are to develop an integrative system of values that we

give up pretending to show respect for authorities that inhibit change by repressing unrestrained enquiry.[1]

This new orthodoxy is presented as universal in its scope, but Andrew Wright suggests reasons why it may prove to be a rather short-lived provincial fashion, confined to this phase of Western culture. It is certain that the new orthodoxy can only become a new establishment by radically distorting the Christian spiritual tradition. The accent in so much modern discussion of spirituality is on the passage from dependence to independence in which the child is freed from constraint in order to construct a reality founded on personal preferences. The tradition of Christian Trinitarian spirituality also involves a passage from dependence to independence but one that is undertaken as a preparation for committed interdependence. In the Christian tradition freedom is for relationship rather than freedom from constraint.

Andrew Wright makes a powerful case for a more genuine pluralism in religious education. It cannot be proper to use state schools to indoctrinate pupils either with some narrow confessionalism or with ironic scepticism. The educational task has to be to develop the spiritual literacy of individuals and of society as a whole by doing justice to the diversity of living traditions.

It may be a shock to some people in the Church of England that the author believes that 'it is perhaps in denominational schools, particularly Anglican ones, that the danger of pupils being nurtured in unsatisfactory modes of spirituality is most prevalent.' I will not spoil the effect by attempting to summarise the argument of Andrew Wright's stimulating final chapter, but I do hope that his book will be widely read and studied. The All Saints Educational Trust can be justly proud of being associated with this publication.

✢ Richard Londin

---

[1] *Education, Spirituality and the Whole Child*, ed. Ron Best, Cassell, 1996.

Introduction

The Enlightenment gave birth to a modern Western culture in which the realms of fact and value were torn apart. Western society found itself living in a context marked by rationalism, materialism and the displacement of faith in ultimate spiritual truth. The romantic reaction to this spiritual sterility sought to recover for humankind a lost dimension of spiritual value. However, the influence of modernity prevailed, and the realm of spiritual experience recovered by romanticism remained individualistic, isolated and dislocated from the wisdom of tradition and community. The children of romanticism were forced to trust their own inner experiences, to learn to judge and discern on the basis of their own innate ability. In time this rootless romantic spirituality was taken up and adopted by post-modern culture. Here there was no ultimate truth, no right or wrong, no point of value beyond individual preference, inclination and desire. Consequently the cultivation of spiritual sensibility became no more than the stimulation of children's ability to adapt themselves to the task of playing freely in a post-modern cultural playground. Deprived of spiritual roots and the skills of spiritual discernment, they became prey to manipulation by the cultural, political and economic powers operating in contemporary society.

This report traces the contours of this story in detail. Part One describes the development of official government policy regarding spiritual education (Chapter One); traces its emergent pedagogic structures within religious education (Chapter Two); and shows how these have come to pervade the whole curriculum (Chapter Three). Part Two offers a constructive critique of this perspective, which reflects a localised spiritual tradition with no claim to universal validity. The connections between modernity, romanticism and post-modernity are drawn out (Chapter Four); and this specific spiritual tradition is contrasted with an alternative, that of Trinitarian Christianity (Chapter Five). Part Three explores the implications of this critique, offering a revised definition of spirituality capable of doing justice to the diversity of spiritual traditions (Chapter

Six); and advocating a spiritual education grounded in the twin notions of cultural roots and spiritual discernment (Chapter Seven).

This report was sponsored by the All Saints Educational Trust. I am grateful to the School of Education and Faculty of Theology at King's College for making available to me the time and resources necessary for the research. Dr Andrew Walker provided invaluable support and encouragement. A number of my research students, in particular Gye Kwang Cho, Janet Brannigan-Croggon and Hergen Haye, took part in discussions that helped develop my thinking in crucial areas. I am indebted to ongoing conversations with Andrew Angel, Jo Backus at Bath College of Higher Education, Jonathan Galloway, and Angela Wright at the London Institute of Education. Needless to say, responsibility for what follows is my own.

Andrew Wright

Part One

Survey:
The Contemporary Consensus

1. Background and Sources

This study of the spiritual dimension of education takes as its frame of reference schooling in England and Wales from 1977 to the present. During this period spirituality has emerged as a key theme in educational theory and practice.

The Evolution of Educational Policy

The roots of the contemporary debate are of relatively recent origin. The 1944 Education Act[1] referred explicitly to spirituality: 'The statutory system of public education ... contributes towards the spiritual, moral, mental and physical development of the community'. However, it seems clear

- that the concept was not in any way central to the legislator's thinking;

- that for some this implied a direct reference to Christianity;

- that for others it suggested an attempt to identify a common set of values upon which education should be founded;

- that the ambiguity of the term reflected a pragmatic concern that the legislation did not over stipulate. [2]

In any case, the concept played little – if any – significant role within educational debate until its re-emergence in 1977. In a speech at Ruskin College in October 1976[3] the Prime Minister, James Callaghan, addressed the fundamental questions of the nature and purpose of education, opening

---

[1] HMSO (1944), Preamble, Part 2, Section 7.

[1] cf. Alves (1991); Gilliat (1996); Maclure (1968); Priestley (1985); Souper & Kay (1982).

[3] Callaghan (1976); cf. Flude & Hammer (1990).

up a debate that culminated in the legislation of the Education Reform Act of 1988.[4] The government's proposals for educational reform were outlined in 1977 in the Green Paper *Education in Our Schools*.[5] It advocated the establishment of a core curriculum, together with the formulation of a set of basic educational aims.

It was the contribution of Her Majesty's Inspectors to this debate that placed the issue of spiritual education firmly on the agenda. Their discussion paper *Curriculum 11–16* [6] argued that education should be concerned with introducing pupils to certain essential areas of human knowledge and experience: aesthetic and creative, ethical, linguistic, mathematical, physical, scientific, social and political, and spiritual. A supplement, responding to requests for further clarification, offered two contrasting definitions of the spiritual area of experience.[7] The first of these was anthropological in its focus.

> The spiritual area is concerned with the awareness a person has of those elements in existence and experience which may be defined in terms of inner feelings and beliefs; they affect the way people see themselves and throw light for them on the purpose and meaning of life itself. Often these feelings and beliefs lead people to claim to know God and glimpse the transcendent; sometimes they represent that striving and longing for perfection which characterises human beings, but always they are concerned with matters at the heart and root of existence.

The second was theological.

> The spiritual area is concerned with everything in human knowledge or experience that is connected with or derives from a sense of God or of gods. Spirituality is a meaningless adjective for the atheist and of dubious use to the agnostic. Irrespective of personal belief or disbelief, an unaccountable number of people have believed and do believe in the

---

4 HMSO (1988); on the religious legislation and its significance cf. Hull (1989), Cox & Cairns (1989).

5 DES (1977).

6 DES / HMI (1977a).

7 DES / HMI (1977b).

spiritual aspects of human life, and therefore their actions, attitudes and interpretations of events have been influenced accordingly.[8]

There was a significant contrast between *Education in Our Schools* and the proposals of HMI. The former assumed a traditional pedagogy that had long dominated British educational practice, one nurtured within the traditions of grammar and public schooling prior to its partial eclipse with the emergence of progressive child-centred education in the 1960s. Its origins are to be found in the education philosophy propounded by John Locke in the seventeenth century.[9] Here the various subject disciplines within the curriculum are studied not as an end in themselves, but rather as the means of achieving the broader aim of the moral development of children.[10] Within this tradition the core curriculum was to operate instrumentally as a tool for inducting children into the broader values of the nation, as defined in statements concerning the fundamental aims of schooling.

In contrast HMI – influenced by the work of Paul Hirst[11] – sought to transcend what was regarded as an essentially parochial notion of education, one limited to the mere transmission of the relative moral norms of a particular culture. In its place was proposed a pedagogy grounded in the objective and universal nature of knowledge.[12] Here learning was ascribed an intrinsic value requiring no external justification or support.

---

[8] ibid.

[9] Locke (1968), (1989); cf. Bantock (1980), pp.245ff; Wright (1995), pp.75f.

[10] Locke (1968): 'a sound mind in a sound body, is a short, but full description of a happy state in this world,' p.114; 'to have the knowledge of a man of business, a carriage suitable to his rank, and to be eminent and useful in his country according to his station' are the marks of an educated gentleman, achieved through an upbringing in which learning leads to virtue, wisdom and breeding, p.197. Bantock, op. cit., observes a 'tension between his humanistic views of conduct and manners and his new "scientific" conception of understanding and utility', pp.245f.

[11] Hirst (1965); Hirst & Peters (1970); cf. Barrow & White (1993).

[12] For Hirst, op. cit., liberal education is constituted by 'an education based fairly and squarely on the nature of knowledge itself,' p.11; compare Newman (1919); for critical discussion of Hirst's developing understanding of the nature of knowledge cf. Evers (1987); Green (1985); Griffiths (1986); Hindess (1972); O'Connor (1972); Scarlett (1984); Smith (1981); Wright, op. cit., pp.249–273; cf. also Hirst (1972), (1973), (1982).

The moral agenda was located firmly within the material content of the curriculum, the achievement of moral knowledge and wisdom being inherent in the learning process itself. The traditional division between that which is taught and the reasons for teaching was thus eradicated: moral education was identified as an ingrained part of the learning process, rather than as a secondary goal towards which teaching should aspire.

If successive policy documents between 1977 and 1988 adopted Hirst's language of 'forms of knowledge' and 'areas of experience', they did so only rhetorically. Such knowledge and experience was quickly identified with the traditional subject disciplines.[13] As a result the substance of HMI's proposals was left on one side: the implementation of a common core curriculum was understood in traditionalist terms as the means to a broader moral end. The *Swann Report* reinforced this strategy, suggesting that the primary merit of Religious Education lay in its potential as an instrument for promoting multi-cultural harmony, rather than in any value the study of religion might have in its own right.[14]

When the 1988 Education Reform Act reached the statute books it was this traditionalist framework that provided its basic structures. The material content of education was to be formed by a subject-focused 'Basic Curriculum', consisting of Religious Education and the disciplines contained within the 'National Curriculum'. This package was to be encompassed within the 'Whole Curriculum', which included cross-curricular themes that served as a bridge between the disciplines and the fundamental moral aims of education which they were to serve. Pupils were to be taught a balanced and broadly based curriculum in such a way that it:

- 'promotes the spiritual, moral, cultural, mental and physical development of pupils at the school and of society' and

- 'prepares such pupils for the opportunities, responsibilities and experiences of adult life.'[15]

This had important ramifications for spiritual education. In the initial HMI proposal the spiritual dimension constituted a body of knowledge and

---

13 DES (1979), (1981), (1985a), (1985b), (1987); DES/HMI (1980); HMSO (1986).

14 HMSO (1985).

15 HMSO (1988), Part 1, Chapter 1:1:2, p.1.

experience that pupils should be taught to investigate and understand. In the 1988 legislation the spiritual dimension was removed from the body of the curriculum and included within the basic statement of educational aims. Spirituality thus came to form a fundamental end of education – as the spiritual development of pupils and society – to which the whole schooling process should direct itself. It was no longer presented as an object of critical study, but as a dimension of human experience permeating the whole of education.

This traditionalist division between aims and curriculum content was reinforced in 1992 by the White Paper *Choice and Diversity*, which stressed the connection between spirituality and those shared values underpinning the ethos and activity of schools.[16] In its 1993 publication *Spiritual and Moral Development*[17] the National Curriculum Council confirmed this perspective. Drawing on the first – anthropological – definition provided by HMI in 1977, it understood spirituality as fundamental to the human condition, transcending ordinary everyday experience and concerned with the search for identity and meaning in response to death, suffering, beauty and evil. Spiritual development was seen in terms of eight aspects: beliefs; the sense of awe, wonder and mystery; feelings of transcendence; the search for meaning and purpose; self-knowledge; relationships; creativity; feelings and emotions. The promotion of spirituality required the nurturing of curiosity, imagination, insight and intuition through the school's ethos, collective worship and explicit curriculum. The final move in the development of policy was the decision of OFSTED to monitor and evaluate the way in which schools responded to their legal obligation to develop the spiritual dimension of pupils and of society.[18] In doing so, it adopted the broad consensus framework as articulated by the NCC.

---

[16] DFE (1992).

[17] NCC (1993), republished as SCAA (1995b).

[18] OFSTED (1993), (1994a), (1994b); cf. SCAA (1994a); cf. also, Grove (1993), Parker (1995), Trainor (1995); note the contrast with earlier uncertainty regarding the possibility of the inspection and evaluation of the spiritual dimension, APU (1981).

The Spiritual Crisis of Modernity

The requirement that schools should promote spiritual development could easily have been reduced to mere rhetoric, resulting in little reflection or practice. Instead, the 1988 legislation engendered a wide-ranging debate and a diversity of practical responses. This result was linked to the widespread perception of a spiritual crisis within society. Prime Minister Callaghan's call for a reappraisal of educational values reflected this concern, one given added urgency by the new Conservative administration. The utilitarian approach to wealth creation through managerial and technological efficiency appeared – at least to those opposed to government policy – to threaten the values and fabric of the welfare society. The inherent weakness of the Labour opposition meant that special interest groups, the trade unions, and even on occasion the churches, found themselves at the forefront of political opposition.[19] Political lobbying and industrial disputes reflected an increasing tendency for active resistance to descend into violence, against the background of inner-city riots and an escalation of the cold war. As the politics of conviction replaced those of consensus, so the political spectrum polarised. The collapse of any middle-ground accord,[20] coupled with the increase in social tension and civil strife, resulted in a commonly held perception of a spiritual vacuum within society. Whether this was understood as the result of the legacy of socialism or as the emergence of a reactionary conservatism, it could no longer be ignored.

This situation of spiritual unease nurtured the re-emergence in the 1980s of the romantic counter-culture of the 1960s. This took the guise of a diversity of New Age movements, now able to draw on the intellectual resources of post-modern philosophy.[21] Claims that any universal system, whether political or religious, might be capable of answering the needs and anxieties of contemporary society were met with increasing scepticism. Cultural diversity, exemplified by the exploration of alternative lifestyles, became the order of the day. Perceptions of spiritual malaise extended from the immediate political context to embrace a growing conviction that the entire heritage of modern Western culture embodied fundamental

---

[19] Clark (1993).

[20] The emergence of the Social Democratic Party, and its subsequent demise, reflects this failure of consensus politics during this period.

[21] Agger (1991), (1992); Giroux (1994); King (1993); Rorty (1989); Usher & Edwards (1994).

flaws. The variety of New Age religious and secular perspectives was held up as evidence of a renewed spiritual hunger, and as an opportunity for recovering a lost dimension of human experience.[22]

Such critiques of modern post-Enlightenment culture are not new: they form part of an extensive historical tradition. Attacks on the legacy of the Enlightenment first emerged in the second half of the eighteenth century and have continued to appear in a variety of different forms.[23] For Rousseau, 'everything is good as it comes from the hands of the maker; everything degenerates in the hands of man.'[24] The experience of the First World War effectively destroyed the Enlightenment's grand narrative of the evolution of rational, moral, enlightened humanity.[25] This was later reinforced by the stark facts of Auschwitz, Hiroshima and Dresden, and later of Vietnam, Cambodia and most recently the former state of Yugoslavia.[26]

The debate surrounding the heritage of the Enlightenment contrasts its emancipatory promise with its transparent failure: 'mankind, instead of entering into a truly human condition, is sinking into a new kind of

---

[22] cf. King (1985): 'Looking at contemporary society in a world context, as we must, we perceive a profound paradox between growing diversity and tension on one hand and the genuine search for integration and a new wholeness on the other ... a new interest in religiousness is apparent although it is often found at the margin or outside established religions. This transformation of contemporary religious consciousness is visible in many areas, not least in the new religious movements ... those who are sufficiently perceptive and reflective can recognise many signs of a spiritual hunger and quest.' p.136.

[23] Note here the convergence and contrast between the critique of modernity offered by the neo-Marxist critical theory of the Frankfurt School, and that of orthodox Trinitarian Christian theologians: Adorno & Horkheimer (1972); Gunton (1985), (1993); Habermas (1987a), (1987b); Hauerwas (1995); Held (1990); Newbigin (1986); Wiggershaus (1995).

[24] Rousseau (1986), p.56, following the translation of Bowen (1981), p.187.

[25] The second edition of Karl Barth's commentary on *Romans*, T.S. Eliot's *The Waste Land*, Kafka's *The Trial* and *The Castle*, Thomas Mann's *The Magic Mountain*, and Stravinsky's revision of *La Sacre du printemps* all appeared between 1922 and 1926; Barth (1980); Eliot (1974); Kafka (1953), (1957); Mann (1960),

[26] cf. e.g., Adorno & Horkheimer op. cit.; Levi (1979), (1989); Rubenstein (1966); Rubenstein & Roth (1987); Simon (1978a), (1978b).

barbarism.'[27] In this context Foucault cautions the tradition of secular humanism: 'You may have killed God beneath the weight of all that you have said; but don't imagine that, with all that you are saying, you will make a man that will live longer than he.'[28]

Neither the belief that humanity is facing a spiritual crisis, nor the identification of modern culture as a significant contributory factor, is particularly original. Both, however, have played significant roles in stimulating and focusing the contemporary educational debate.

The Spiritual Crisis in Education

The broad educational debate, informed by the emergent legislation, draws directly on this perception of spiritual crisis, both reflecting and responding to it. Despite the diversity of standpoints and perspectives informing the discussion, a number of core themes are continually repeated.

Modern culture has put its faith in the sterile rationalism of science and the authority of political and religious ideology, and as a result it has placed itself at the mercy of power structures that serve to constrain human freedom. The roots of this spiritual crisis can be traced back to the Enlightenment's differentiation of the realm of fact from aesthetic, moral and spiritual values. The curriculum of schools and universities – grounded in a dualism between science and the humanities – confirms the existence of a 'logical chasm between ought and is'.[29] This separation of fact from value constitutes the foundation of modern secular consciousness, providing a mythical framework that dominates political and economic structures. For Grimmitt the 'traditional cultures of spirituality ... are marginalised and silenced by the contemporary combination of bureaucracy, industry and the consciousness-creating media'.[30] By ignoring spiritual experience in favour of rational explanations of the natural order, modern education treats physical objects as ends in

---

[27] Adorno & Horkheimer (1972), p.xi.

[28] Foucault (1991), p.211.

[29] Holley (1978), p.53.

[30] Grimmitt (1987), p.120.

themselves and consequently lacks the wisdom to appreciate their 'instrumental value as aids and guides to the spiritual life'.[31]

These failings of modernity are held to be reflected in contemporary schooling. Despite its stress on the central importance of the spiritual dimension, the 1988 Education Reform Act is perceived as a piece of reactionary legislation that 'bids fair to reinforce narrowly discipline-based approaches and instrumental economy-driven objectives.'[32] The National Curriculum's affirmation of distinct subject disciplines reflects a reductive education that emphasises the objective, rational, empirical and descriptive in preference to the perspectives, experiences and needs of pupils.[33] This leads to a pedagogy concerned with social utility, vocational value and wealth creation.[34] As a result the intrinsic spiritual value of humanity is undermined: for Hill the focus 'on the satisfaction of material needs without sufficient regard for the spiritual nature and needs of human beings ... can lead to people becoming trapped in consumerism, naive about the political forces which manipulate them, and exploitative in human relationships.'[35] The Act's legislation regarding Religious Education, cross-curricular dimensions and themes and spirituality is for Priestley a mere afterthought that attempts to disguise an implicit materialistic metaphysic. He judges that 'the whole package reeks of hypocrisy.'[36]

This suspicion of traditional forms of education is not new. The rise of progressive child-centred programmes and teaching methods in the 1960s constituted an earlier attempt to protect the spiritual integrity of the individual pupil from erosion by modern culture.[37] Progressivism in turn drew on the intellectual resources of a romantic tradition which can be traced back to Rousseau in the eighteenth century. Central to his

---

[31] Holley (1978), p.49.

[32] Hill (1989), p.174.

[33] Webster (1982b); cf. Priestley (1982a).

[34] Priestley (1992).

[35] Hill op. cit., p.174.

[36] Priestley op. cit., p.30.

[37] Darling (1986); though the language of 'spirituality' was not present in the 1960s, the main concerns of progressive education bear a remarkable similarity to the contemporary spirituality debate.

educational philosophy was the affirmation of the natural goodness of children, coupled with a belief that such goodness is inevitably corrupted by contact with civilisation.[38] Against this background the 1988 Education Reform Act has been interpreted as a reactionary attempt to recover a traditional subject-centred model of education and thereby counter the influence of progressive education.

Although the term 'spirituality' was given currency by the debate leading to the 1988 Education Reform Act, its precise meaning remains open to interpretation. Defenders of the increasingly isolated tradition of romantic education have seized this opportunity to make the language of spirituality their own, interpreting it in terms of a child-centred agenda and thereby retaining a foothold for progressivism within mainstream educational debate. References to spirituality increasingly represent rallying points around which opposition to traditional subject-centred education can gather.

Phenix offers a classic example of this process. He suggests that the re-emergence of traditional subject-centred education reflects a fundamental imbalance between personal and conceptual knowledge.[39] Modern education gives priority to conceptual, discursive, and academic forms of understanding: 'in our literate culture it is commonly assumed that conceptual knowledge is the best kind, the only kind really worthy of being called knowledge.'[40] This, however, is a fundamental error, since 'students immersed in a world of autonomous concepts feel alienated and impoverished ... expected to live in a world of ideas that is out of touch with their own personal existence ... [they] lose any sense of vital meaning in their studies.'[41] Phenix contrasts this with a notion of personal knowledge that he believes is undermined by the modern education system. This form of knowledge involves the whole person and is expressed primarily in action rather than passive reflection. It is grounded in an immediate grasp of reality, a primal sense of knowing, experienced

---

[38] Rousseau (1986) argues that 'the first impulses of nature are always right; there is no original sin in the human heart,' consequently authentic education consists 'not in teaching virtue or truth, but in preserving the heart from vice and from the spirit of error,' pp.56f.

[39] Phenix (1982); cf. Maxwell (1987); Polanyi (1958).

[40] Phenix op. cit., p.12.

[41] ibid., p.14.

directly in one's inner being unmediated by the sterile structures of academic learning. The educated person bears witness to the existential truth of his or her existence through authentic living. For Phenix, spiritual education must redress the current educational imbalance by making such personal knowledge the benchmark against which conceptual knowledge must be tested. He thus points the way towards an organic and holistic educational programme, one capable of stimulating the imagination to address ultimate questions[42] and enabling pupils to recover a sense of awe in their encounters with the strangeness and immensity of reality.[43] For Priestley such a policy confirms the truth of Whitehead's dictum that 'the essence of education is that it be religious.'[44]

Regeneration through Spiritual Education

Thus the contemporary debate regarding the task of spiritual education, developing in the context of the evolution of official government policy and against the background of perceptions of a spiritual crisis within society, reflects a concern to recover the progressive insights that dominated educational practice in the 1960s. The recognition of education's complicity in the spiritual decadence and poverty of society is coupled with a belief that education can contribute to the resolution of the crisis.

Initially this discussion was almost exclusively the preserve of Religious Education, with Holley's 1978 monograph[45] providing the benchmark for a series of studies that appeared, with increasing regularity, from the early 1980s onwards. By the time the 1988 Education Reform Act entered the statute books the debate had expanded to embrace other curriculum areas, cross-curricular themes, pastoral care and whole school policy.[46] Despite a widespread belief that spirituality is by its very nature an elusive entity that defies adequate conceptualisation, a survey of the relevant literature during the last twenty years reveals a remarkable degree of uniformity.

---

[42] Priestley (1992).

[43] cf. Webster (1982a).

[44] Priestley op. cit., p.27; Whitehead (1970).

[45] Holley (1978).

[46] cf. e.g. Best (1996).

The foundations of this contemporary consensus are grounded in the near unanimous affirmation of the first – anthropological – definition of the spiritual as offered by HMI. The spiritual dimension is thus understood as that area of human awareness, experience and inner feeling that illuminates the purpose and meaning of life, offers a glimpse of transcendence, reflects the longing for perfection, and deals with matters at the heart and root of existence.

The second – theological – definition, with its tighter focus on human knowledge and experience related to a sense of God, carries with it 'such extensive baggage, such a weight of historical and theological meaning,' that it is generally regarded as unsuitable.[47] Any attempt to restore the spiritual by restoring religion cannot be considered as a viable option.[48] Indeed, the narrow exclusivity of the theological definition is held to be inherently dangerous, offering up the spectre of educational apartheid.[49] Spirituality needs to be hauled out of its traditional ecclesiastical setting, out of its grottoes and ghettos, into the contemporary world.[50] Only the anthropological definition, with its universal vision open to all regardless of their religious persuasion, can achieve this.[51] 'The notion of "spiritual" continues to be meaningful to more people than does the term "religious".'[52] The all-embracing nature of the definition is held to reflect its potential as a resource for human development, offering a path towards the recovery of meaning and purpose in which 'knowledge opens on to what is ultimately mysterious.'[53]

This affirmation of the anthropological definition reflects the assumption, legislated for by the 1988 Act, that spirituality is to be understood not as an object of study within the curriculum, but as the all-pervading context within which education operates. Here the need is not to identify a diversity of spiritual traditions that might form the subject of investigation in the classroom, but rather to articulate a common universal definition

---

[47] Webster (1993), p.130.

[48] Grimmitt (1987), pp.167–193.

[49] Rudge (1994).

[50] Lealman (1986).

[51] cf. Grove (1993).

[52] Priestley (1985), p.114.

[53] Webster (1982b), p.80.

into which all pupils may be inducted. From a political perspective, the issue is whether the spiritual context of education should be grounded within the mainstream Christian heritage of the nation, or reflect the religiously plural context of contemporary society. The acceptance of HMI's anthropological definition represents a defeat for conservative attempts to reaffirm the mainstream Christian roots of society in favour of a liberal affirmation of religious diversity.[54]

Thus the examination of the background and sources of the contemporary debate reveal the evolution of official policy regarding spiritual education; a growing perception of a spiritual crisis in contemporary culture, which is reflected in education; and the emergent belief that spiritual education should provide a remedial response to spiritual decay.

---

[54] Burn & Hart (1988); Hart (1994); cf. Brown (1995).

2. Religious Education and Spirituality

Government policy developed against the background of a society in spiritual crisis; education sought to discharge itself from complicity in this situation and provide a remedial response to spiritual decay, and it was in the domain of Religious Education that this strategy first emerged. This debate began in the early 1980s, predating the cross-curricular discussions that flourished after 1988. This chapter sets out to outline the basic contours of Religious Education's programme for spiritual education.

The Task of Religious Education

Ever since the early 1960s Religious Education's place within the modern education system has been equivocal. The plurality of religious traditions, coupled with secular suspicion of religion, led to charges of indoctrination and doubts whether the subject could justify its place within an open liberal educational context. This resulted in a curriculum development programme driven primarily by the desire to achieve public consensus at the expense of any recognition of the diversity and ambiguity of religion. The 'objective' phenomenological description of religion offered a way into the plurality of world faiths: by suspending all questions of religious truth, it managed to avoid any hint of religious confessionalism. This search for consensus influenced the spirituality debate. The option of using the tensions between the two HMI definitions to explore the pluralistic heritage of spirituality, thus enabling pupils to grapple with the ambiguity of diverse and contradictory religious and secular stances, was never seriously considered. If spirituality was to constitute the end rather than the content of education, then the central task was the establishment of agreement regarding the nature of that particular educational objective. Thus Lealman posed the question, 'Can people who approach education from different philosophical/theological viewpoints find a common working definition?'[1] When the issue was approached in this manner, the choice of the general anthropological definition offered by HMI, rather than the narrower theological formulation, was clearly irresistible.

Alongside the drive to achieve consensus stood the desire to demonstrate the relevance of Religious Education. This had been a central issue ever since Loukes drew attention to the gulf between religion and the everyday experiences of the vast majority of children.[2] The implicit Religious Education of the 1960s was fundamentally concerned with the attempt to bridge this gap between religious language and children's experience. The phenomenological Religious Education of the 1970s was similarly motivated when it drew the distinction between religious description and empathetic understanding. Religious Education thus adopted a dualistic distinction between the irrelevance that springs from the objectification of external religious culture, and the relevance of the subjective perception and internalisation of religious meaning. Cox's classic distinction between 'understanding religion' and 'religious understanding', and SCAA's contrast between 'learning about' and 'learning from' religion, demonstrate this clearly.[3] Indeed, Day found that the subject's inability to reconcile these two approaches suggested that it suffered from a permanent identity crisis.[4] The phenomenological framework that dominated Religious Education in the 1970s represented a swing of the pendulum from the 'subjective yet personally relevant' to the 'objective but personally irrelevant'. The subsequent emphasis on spirituality and the adoption of the anthropological definition allowed Religious Education to reaffirm its relevance in the lives of children.

The structures of Religious Education thus demanded an approach to spirituality grounded in the principles of consensus and relevance. As a result the adoption of the anthropological definition marked a natural step forward. The findings of empirical research into the nature and provenance of religious spiritual experience supported and consolidated this move. Operating within a tradition instigated by William James (1842–1910), Alister Hardy and Edward Robinson at the Religious Experience Research Unit at Oxford, together with analogous work carried out by David Hay at

---

[1] Lealman (1986), p.67.

[2] Loukes (1961).

[3] Cox (1983); SCAA (1994b).

[4] Day (1985).

Nottingham University, produced results that struck a public chord that resonated far beyond the boundaries of Religious Education.[5] The results of such research offered striking evidence of the widespread occurrence of religious experience. Participants attributed immense value to a range of spiritual encounters that transcend the formal boundaries of religious communities. It was within the framework of the anthropological definition that such research findings could best be interpreted. Such evidence served to reinforce the sense of the universality and relevance of the spiritual dimension within the subject.

Religious Education thus used spiritual experience as a way of bringing consensus and relevance to the study of religion. The adoption of an experiential–expressive model of religion allowed the subject to highlight the spiritual dimension: primary spiritual experience is expressed in the secondary cultural phenomena of the various religious traditions. This specific interpretative framework, with its roots in nineteenth-century liberal Protestant theology, gave priority to subjective experience over the accidental trappings of religious culture. If pupils were to learn 'from' rather than merely 'about' religion, then they must pass beyond the external manifestations of religious expression and enter into its experiential heart. The parallels between the anthropological definition of spirituality and this experiential–expressive model of religion are transparent. Spiritual education, embracing the subjective concerns and values of pupils, served to supplement the tradition of phenomenological Religious Education and at the same time reinforce the subject's search for consensus and relevance.

A concern to justify this adoption of the experiential–expressive paradigm does not feature significantly in the literature. Priestley's work is in part an exception, displaying an awareness of its historical roots in the nineteenth-century liberal Protestant theology of Otto and Schleiermacher, and of the links between this theology and the broad romantic tradition that nurtured it. He thus comes face to face with the romantic critique of modernity offered by Whitehead, Coleridge, Wordsworth and others. This is precisely the tradition from which progressive education's critique of the modern tendency towards objectification developed. The alliance between educational progressivism and the experiential–expressive model of

---

[5] Hardy (1966), (1979); Hay (1974), (1977), (1982a), (1982b), (1985), (1990); Hay, Nye & Murphy (1996); James (1960); Nye (1996); Nye & Hay (1996); Robinson (1977a), (1977b), (1978).

religion offered a common framework for spiritual education: both sought to recover subjective sensibility from the tyranny of modern objectivism. Significantly, Priestley fails to go on to analyse this romantic critique of modernity, choosing rather to assume that simply identifying its historical roots and affirming its continuity with contemporary educational debate constitutes a justification in itself.

The significance of spirituality for the status of Religious Education as a discipline was enormous. Here was a public debate at the heart of the educational system upon which religious educators could speak with authority. After years of fighting a rear-guard action to establish its universal credentials and public relevance, the possibility of a pro-active strategy emerged. Religious Education, through its contribution to spiritual education, saw the opportunity to move beyond the need to accommodate itself within the prevailing modern culture, towards a policy of effective challenge and revision of the status quo. The task of attending to the spiritual dimension of Religious Education, understood within the broad anthropological framework, was seen as universal in scope and of immediate relevance in the lives of pupils.

The Representation of Religion

In attending to the task of spiritual education, Religious Education was to represent religion in the classroom in a form capable of stimulating spiritual insight. The adoption of the anthropological definition provided the necessary sense of universality and relevance demanded by this strategy.

However, the rejection of HMI's theological definition of spirituality was not without its problems. How were theological approaches to spirituality, those 'stamped by the decision of faith',[6] to be handled? What of Berryman's presupposition that 'the child's spirituality is assumed to be a comprehensive relationship with God that involves the whole person in an ultimate way'?[7] Where were the distinctive spiritualities rooted in specific faith traditions, such as the belief that 'at the centre of Christian spirituality lies that insight into God which is revealed by Jesus Christ and which is interpreted by the Holy Spirit,'[8] to be located within the curriculum?

---

6 Webster (1993), p.134.

7 Berryman (1985), p.120.

8 Webster op. cit., p.134.

Ignoring such traditions would bypass an extraordinarily rich vein of spirituality; yet affirming them would threaten a return to a narrow confessionalism at odds with the need to maintain consensus and relevance.

The solution to this dilemma was to accommodate the various theological spiritualities within the anthropological framework, though ultimately this entailed a reduction of their theological content. The first step in this process was to draw a distinction between religion and spirituality. The spiritual domain transcends the limited sphere of religion and is independent of any form of religious belief; consequently spiritual experience may occur apart from religious traditions.[9] Thus Holley suggests 'that man does conceptualise ultimate reality – in terms such as God, Allah, Brahman – and does thereby direct his affections cannot be denied. But the idea that such a conceptualisation is the sum total of ultimate spiritual reality is once again irreligious.'[10]

Given the priority of the spiritual over the religious, it becomes possible to distinguish between authentic manifestations of religion (which serve to enhance the spiritual domain) and inauthentic ones (which tend to extinguish genuine spirituality). Religion, in its inauthentic form, takes on a pathological function as an instrument of religious ideology. Here corrupt institutionalised religious structures abuse the authentic spiritual roots of religious traditions. The line of demarcation between authentic and inauthentic religion lies in the distinction between religious experience and religious expression.[11] It is not enough simply to define religion merely as observable phenomena; rather its essence is that dimension of religious experience, awareness and sensibility that precedes any cultural expression. Primary religious experience leads into secondary religious expression. It is necessary to see 'the historical faiths as the cultural expression of personal religious experience'.[12]

This introduction of the experiential–expressive model is portrayed as consistent with the self-understanding of the various religious communities, despite the obvious tensions with a variety of notions of

---

[9] Lealman (1986), p.66.

[10] Holley (1978), p.60.

[11] Hay (1982a).

[12] ibid., p.48; Hay is drawing on the religious sociology of Wach and the liberal theology of Schleiermacher; Schleiermacher (1958), (1976); Wach (1958), (1962).

revelation. Thus Hay speaks of the need to 'present religion as what it claims to be, the response of human beings to what they experience as the sacred', and asserts that this position 'of course is a totally orthodox and traditional way of looking at it.'[13]

Religious experience is expressed through linguistic traditions and it is vital that the value of such traditions is not ignored, provided that they retain an authentic relationship with the original experience. 'Without the availability of a complex and subtle theoretical framework, our knowledge remains in a dangerous state of chaotic uncertainty.'[14] Nevertheless, the traditions of religious expression are ultimately of secondary importance. Religious language functions as symbolic metaphor through which an image from the external world illuminates the inner dimension of spirituality: 'metaphor holds within itself familiar, unfamiliar, ordinary and transcendent; it communicates its meaning indirectly; its meaning has to be explored, searched out, reflected on.'[15] Lealman introduces here a distinction between concept and symbol:[16] religious language provides not conceptual descriptions of objective reality, but symbolic expressions of subjective experience. To ignore this truth is to fall into a modernist objectification of religion that leads to inauthentic belief by destroying its spiritual potential. The process of learning to use religious language correctly 'may well involve an intellectual awareness of the world outside but it does so *for the purpose* of evoking the world inside us.'[17]

This perspective is not, as has already been intimated, without its difficulties. It seems apparent that the vast majority of religious traditions understand their narratives, myths, stories, creeds and doctrinal formulations as related to reality itself, however mediated through metaphorical language they might be. Despite the claim that the experiential–expressive model of religion is consistent with the self-understanding of the various faith traditions, a significant undermining of theological realism appears in the literature at this stage. Lealman, for example, is happy to bypass the explicit truth claims of the variety of religious traditions by encouraging pupils to create their own accounts of

---

13 Hay (1982a), p.48.

14 ibid., p.50.

15 Lealman (1982a), p.61.

16 Lealman (1986), p.66.

17 Priestley (1985), p.116, italics original.

reality: 'let there be a shaping of a symbol to represent *what for you* is the reality with which religion is concerned.'[18] Religious symbols, she suggests, may well retain their power and meaning; yet to preserve them to the exclusion of new ones 'would be to deny the place of creative imagination, both in finding new symbols and in giving new interpretations to the old symbols.'[19]

In similar fashion Hay, despite his claim to retain faith with the self-understanding of the faith communities, affirms 'the relativity of all belief systems' and 'the necessity to refer back constantly to our direct experience of the world, as the criterion by which to judge the validity of our beliefs.'[20] Priestley, having defended the thesis that the concept 'God' functions instrumentally within religious stories as a way of evoking a sense of transcendence, goes on to state that 'the constructs, however intellectual they may be, are, in the last analysis, images and, therefore, a product of the human imagination.'[21] He later argues that any eclipse of the creative imagination in favour of 'an insistence on doctrinal orthodoxy and a refusal to countenance any form of heresy is, perhaps quite literally, soul destroying.'[22] Webster, who elsewhere displays a keener sense than most of the tension between religious (in his case specifically Anglican) orthodoxy and the experiential–expressive model, nevertheless invokes Tillich in suggesting that 'in the depth of every living religion there is a point at which the religion itself loses its particularity, elevating it to spiritual freedom.'[23]

The attempt to accommodate theological spirituality within the anthropological perspective is thus dependent on the primacy of abstract spiritual experience over concrete religious formulations. Those theological traditions seeking a home within the anthropological definition must succumb to a process of reinterpretation in which the primary reference of their language is transferred from reality itself to the human experience of reality. The path to religious knowledge now passes directly

---

[18] Lealman (1982b), p.75, my italics.

[19] Lealman (1986), p.66.

[20] Hay (1982a), p.47; drawing on Berger & Luckmann (1967).

[21] Priestley (1985), p.116.

[22] Priestley (1992), p.34.

[23] Tillich (1963) p.95, quoted in Webster (1993), p.138.

through the subjectivity of experience: sensibility becomes the bridge between language and reality. Religious truth will always be felt before it is named, consequently any theological formulation becomes relative, contingent, ambiguous and even arbitrary. The agnostic conclusions that follow are perhaps inevitable. For Lealman the search for transcendence leads us into the 'area of ambiguity, surprise, riddle, of the parable, the Koan – and RE needs, probably more than anything, to exist on a Koan point – that is, for questions to be answered with questions.'[24] She goes on to quote, with approval, Koestler's reference to the thrill of 'a new innocence of perception liberated from the cataract of accepted beliefs.'[25]

The task of stimulating spiritual insight within Religious Education was thus achieved by presenting religious traditions as secondary expressions of primary spiritual experience. This required a distinction between authentic and pathological expressions of such experience, and demanded that specific theological traditions be interpreted within a generic experiential–expressive framework, despite the dangers of reductionism that accompanied such a procedure.

The Instrumental Function of Religion

The experiential–expressive model presented religion in the classroom in a form capable of stimulating spiritual perception. As a result, the process of studying religion now became a functional one. In this, although the importance of the faith traditions is recognised, their investigation is not seen as an end in itself: 'it is necessary to develop the ability to pinpoint the insights and religious experience the traditions indicate and to use these in the process of identifying and interpreting personal religious experience.'[26] If there is 'a balance to be struck between knowing and understanding the experiences of others and using that knowledge to know and understand ourselves', it nevertheless remains true that 'the great purpose of education should be to give people a greater reliance on the validity of their own inward and private experience.'[27]

---

[24] Lealman (1982a), p.62.

[25] ibid. The quotation is from Koestler's *The Sleepwalker*, though Lealman fails to provide a full reference.

[26] Lealman (1982b), p.77.

[27] Priestley (1992), p.35.

From this perspective the failure of modern Religious Education lies in the fact that it has not yet been able to fulfil this vision and instead remains trapped within the structures of conceptual knowledge. Religious educators must take their share of responsibility for this, since their willingness to 'adjust the subject to meet the demands of the age' has resulted in 'an academic and empirical approach to religion which is in direct conflict with the subject matter.'[28] Consequently understanding religion requires only a narrow range of learning skills and techniques: acquiring knowledge, amassing facts and remembering intellectual propositions. 'The excessive objectification of religious education proposed by the advocates of the phenomenological approach, in which questions of personal values, commitments and beliefs are safely bracketed out, fails to recognise the centrality of pupil's own inwardness in the learning process.'[29] Further, 'the emphasis on the desirability of academic detachment ... has had the effect of disengaging pupils at a personal level from what they are studying.'[30] Driven by the fear of accusations of indoctrination, teachers have failed in their moral duty to educate pupils 'in', rather than merely 'about', their subject.[31]

The development of this critical perspective has produced 'clear signs of unease with the notion of religious education as the phenomenological study of religions and a movement towards a more pupil-centred, personalistic approach.'[32] This requires the rejection of mere academic rationalism, the recovery of the dimension of transcendence that has its reference point beyond modern reductive accounts of humanity,[33] and a 'move beyond an objective study of religions to an exploration of inwardness, a grappling with existential questions, a search for spiritual identity, an encounter with mystery and transcendence.'[34]

Religious Education's rejection of its modernist past through the turn to spiritual education parallels the progressive attack on the subject-centred

---

[28] Priestley (1982a), pp.5f.

[29] Slee (1992), p.40.

[30] Watson (1993a), p.73.

[31] cf. Hudson (1982).

[32] Bates (1982), p.32.

[33] Priestley, op. cit.

[34] Slee, op. cit., p.42.

structures of the 1988 Education Reform Act. The alliance between progressive educators and religious educators interprets the crisis of modern society, and the schooling that flows from it, in terms of the need for a spiritual education that is capable of challenging and undermining the limitations of modernity.

Hay has provided the clearest account of the need for a direct confrontation with modern secular censorship and its hermeneutic of suspicion directed towards spiritual experience.[35] The modernist belief that the sense of the sacred represents a pathological illusion leads to the suppression of the sublime and denial of transcendence. Though Hay produces hard evidence for the ability of spiritual experience to resist the corrosive function of modernity, he retains a generally pessimistic outlook that is acutely conscious of the enormity of the task that lies ahead. King offers a far more optimistic picture of the possibility of the recovery of the lost spiritual dimension. She finds clear 'signs today that the heritage of an empirical and positivist approach to knowledge and experience is faltering and that a new religious sense, atrophied for so long, is being born ... whether in the writings and examples of the saints and mystics of all ages and religions, or in the New Age thinkers and the new physicists today, or in the spiritualities of feminism ... and the peace movement.'[36]

The exploration of religion is thus no longer understood as an end in itself, but instrumentally as a means to a broader end. The adoption of a progressive child-centred agenda means that the task of stimulating inner spiritual awareness has priority over the academic study of the external representations of religious culture.

It was, then, Religious Education that took the lead in formulating a programme for spiritual education. Its task was to demonstrate the relevance and universality of religion by penetrating beyond its culturally bound exterior into its spiritual heart, thereby opening children's minds to the possibility of an authentic spiritual existence. This was to be achieved by presenting religion in the classroom through an experiential–expressive framework in which the subjectivity of internal primary religious experience has priority over the objectivity of external secondary religious expression. As a result, the study of religion was no longer seen as an end

---

[35] Hay (1985).

[36] King (1985), p.139.

in itself, but as a process of instrumental value in stimulating spiritual insight.

3. The Nature of Spiritual Experience

Religious Education's account of the priority of spiritual experience over religious expression understood the former as a universal and essential realm of authentic human existence. This facilitated the application of the perspectives formulated by religious educators across the whole curriculum, in line with the demands of the 1988 Education Reform Act.

Spiritual Experience and Human Nature

It is, according to the discussion outlined in the previous chapter, human experience rather than theological doctrines that constitute the ground of our spirituality. This paves the way for the general acceptance that spiritual experience is – in its purest form – pre-linguistic: divorced from any necessary relationship with language; freed from the constraints of conceptual knowledge. Thus Priestley suggests that 'spiritual awareness manifests itself first of all in feelings and emotions from which it has to be translated into thought if it is to be talked about at all.'[1] There is however no imperative to verbalise such experience since 'it can equally well be expressed in terms of music, art and movement, and even when it is expressed in language, it is likely to be in the form of poetic utterance rather than propositional statement.'[2] Holley describes this dimension of pre-linguistic sensibility as 'creature feeling' that embodies an experience of dependence, infinite freedom, dynamism, and spiritual self-awareness, leading to a 'sense of alienation, of being an exile here on earth, and the desire for liberation from dissatisfying empirical reality.'[3] For Webster it embodies that spark of imaginative self transcendence, reflective of the profoundest depth of human existence, which constitutes the spiritual

---

1 Priestley (1985), p.114; contrast Wright (1996a).

2 Priestley, ibid.

3 Holley (1978), p.58.

category of personal being: 'Its co-ordinates are thought, freedom and creativity; its expression is through commitment, valuation and aspiration.'[4] There is common agreement that the areas of human activity that reflect most accurately this spiritual dimension of experience are those of the expressive and creative arts.[5]

Most descriptions of spiritual experience are content to retain this focus on the inner pre-linguistic experience of individuals. However, there are some attempts to tease out the connections between spiritual experience and the individual's embodied context within linguistic tradition, community, the environment and her or his received cultural traditions. Thus Webster adds to the category of transcendent awareness the following forms of experience: encountering others; social living that is aware of the limitations of one's present intellectual and moral frames of reference; commitment to a principle; awareness of contingency; and hope that the truth lies ahead.[6] This attempt to embody abstract pre-linguistic experience within the flow of communal culture, language and tradition reflects a growing concern – albeit apart from the mainstream of debate – with the inherently dislocated nature of spiritual experience. Hull, for example, has been quick to perceive the dangers of immediate spiritual experience descending into an unrestrained anarchy of subjectivism. He rejects the entire notion that spirituality is the cultivation of an inner journey of discovery and self-transcendence. Such formulations give birth to types of spirituality that are ambiguous and self-deceptive, possessing a tendency to atomise communities, emphasise individuality and heighten competitive awareness of one's own interests.[7]

---

4 Webster (1982b), p.88.

5 Webster, op. cit.; cf. also: Alcock (1993); Attridge (1993); Durka & Smith (1979); Erricker (1993); Gibson (1993); Green (1993); Harris (1988); Jackson (1993); Jenkins (1993); Lealman (1993); Lealman & Robinson (1980), (1981), (1983); Robinson (1982); Slee (1992); Starkings (1993a), (1993b); Wall (1993); Watson (1993b); Yeomans (1993a), (1993b).

6 Webster, op. cit.

7 Hull (1995b); cf. also: Thatcher (1983), (1991), (1996); Wright (1996b). Commenting on the National Curriculum Council's discussion of spirituality, NCC (1993) – cf. SCAA (1995b) – Thatcher (1996) notes that 'the view of the pupil which dominates the document is the individual, autonomous self', and suggests that 'the Enlightenment has bequeathed to us this isolated view of human individuals; the truth is that everything we are we have become through others,

Operating within the tradition of empirical research into religious experience, Hay finds both pre-linguistic and contextualised manifestations of spiritual experience. On the one hand, he identifies occurrences of spontaneous pre-linguistic religious experience in which individuals are surprised by an unexpected awareness of God's presence.[8] Though such experience may be quasi-perceptual, it is common that nothing is perceived through the normal sense organs. On the other hand, there are religious experiences that are contextualised through a direct link with the immediate physical and cultural context.[9] Hay discovers four main forms of such embodied experience:

- experiences of rekindled hierophanies, in which religious or secular ritual sensitises and deepens awareness, serving to remind the believer of the presence of God, often followed by a direct awareness of that presence;

- experiences stimulated by reading scripture;

- experiences of 'life as the language of God', in which a sense of meaning and purpose in events is stimulated by dreams, unusual patterns of experience, or simply the shape of the untidy flow of one's life;

- experiences of prayer, meditation and contemplation.

Thatcher attacks both the centrality given by Hay to the 'inner space' of human subjectivity and also its failure to relate to external reality. Superficially this critique appears misplaced, given Hay's acknowledgement of the contextual nature of much religious experience.[10] However, it gains in authority once the essentially accidental qualities of such contextualisation are recognised. For Hay the cultural and linguistic context is always secondary to the primary decontextualised experience. It functions instrumentally as a contingent stimulus of experience. The nature, quality or legitimacy of the cultural context is not a fundamental issue, and is to be judged merely on a pragmatic or functional level. A

---

and our own "identity" is constituted by relationships, not incidental to them,' p.123.

[8] Hay (1985), p.142.

[9] ibid., pp.142–144.

[10] Hammond, Hay, et al. (1990); Thatcher (1991); Hammond & Hay (1992); Thatcher (1993); Wright (1995) pp.126–132; Mott-Thornton (1996).

sacred place, poem, event, tradition or ritual has value not in itself, but only as it participates in the cycle of the expression of experiences and stimulus of new ones.

The accidental nature of the cultural context of spiritual experience raises the further question of its objective content. Hay here is consistent in his affirmation that when such experience relates to a transcendent object, it does indeed connect humanity with a divine reality. If he hesitates to enter into any substantial detail when describing its nature, this is simply because he holds that the transcendent realm can never be known directly, only ever intuited through our experiences. Hay is thus unambiguous in rejecting any reductionist attempt to limit such experience to mere human projection, wish fulfilment or self-transcendence. He understands Feuerbach's critique of religious experience, which does indeed affirm such a reduction of theology to anthropology, as a reflection of secular suspicion regarding the objectivity of transcendent reality.[11]

Grimmitt's response to Hay at this point sounds a note of hesitancy, counselling against the possibility of returning to a necessary connection between spiritual and religious experience.[12] Further weight is given to this voice of caution by research carried out by Miles.[13] Focusing on the distinction between Paffard's immanent–naturalistic understanding of spiritual experience and Hardy's transcendent–supernaturalistic approach,[14] he finds that, *contra* Hay, those who recognise having received some form of spiritual experience do not necessarily feel the need to invoke religious explanations for it, and yet this does not diminish their perception of its value. He concludes that 'there is a logical gap between accounts of religious experience and the belief that God exists.'[15]

Inner pre-linguistic experience thus appears to mark the focal point of the spiritual. There is no more than an accidental relationship between spiritual experience and the individual's cultural context, and no necessary relationship between such experience and either the affirmation or denial of a divine being that might be held up as its source or point of reference.

---

[11] Feuerbach (1989).

[12] Grimmitt (1987), pp.187–191.

[13] Miles (1994).

[14] Hardy (1966), (1979); Paffard (1973).

[15] Miles, op. cit., p.10.

This being so, it is difficult to avoid the conclusion that ultimately the source of such experience, if it has no necessary connection with either linguistic and cultural tradition or divine reality and revelation, must be human nature itself.

This reading is confirmed by the literature, which implies an anthropology in which the human being is 'primarily a spiritual subject'[16] and the search for spiritual meaning 'a fundamental human activity'.[17] Grimmitt makes this issue explicit: 'in speaking of human spirituality, therefore, I am referring to a human capacity for a certain type of awareness ... the activation of the human capacity for self-transcendence and movement towards a state of consciousness in which the limitations of human finite identity are challenged by the exercise of the creative imagination.'[18] Adopting a neo-Kantian framework, he understands this capacity as a natural one, endowed at birth, a view he regards as parallel to Chomsky's advocacy of natural inborn linguistic competency.[19] It is not possible, he suggests, to reduce this innate capacity merely to the human ability to reason and respond to emotion since 'it challenges the adequacy of that understanding which is solely a product of exercising the intellect or responding to the emotions and provides an alternative understanding of human experience which is the product of neither of these.'[20]

That such natural spiritual competency has not been identified within any empirically supported developmental model of human nature should not come as any surprise, since its very nature is to transcend any such predetermined structures.[21] Even if it cannot be adequately described, such spiritual capacity may nevertheless be understood both as a striving towards the recovery of a primeval purity and innocence of perception,[22] and also as the longing and hope for future perfection. It has an

---

[16] Holley (1978): 'the concept of religion implies an awareness of oneself as primarily a spiritual subject, potentially infinitizable yet dependent and vulnerable', p.59.

[17] Lealman (1982b), p.76.

[18] Grimmitt (1987), p.125.

[19] ibid., p.126.

[20] ibid.

[21] Minney (1995).

[22] Lealman, op. cit.

epistemological function, though this must be sharply distinguished from cognition. Spiritual knowledge has to do with the provocation of awareness, the sharpening of sense perceptions, the stimulation of imagination;[23] with inspiration, creative imagination, the activation of deep inner resources;[24] with the development of the poetic rather than scientific sensibility.[25] Such an epistemology is grounded in intuition and an intense cosmological awareness that functions not as an explanation of the rational order of the world but as a practical mode of life.[26] The spiritual dimension is thus universalised and seen in anthropological terms as an essential aspect of human nature.

Experience, Reality and Truth

If the capacity for spiritual insight and comprehension is fundamental to the human condition, questions inevitably arise about the nature of the reality that is apprehended. What is the proper object of subjective human spirituality? Is there any relationship between spiritual wisdom and how things truly are in the order of things? Does it matter if a child's spiritual insight is contradicted by the actual nature of the universe?

Holley responds to these issues by developing a neo-Kantian ontology that affirms the metaphysical primacy of the spiritual dimension. He takes this realm to be 'the objective reality of the spiritual ultimacy of the cosmos, both essential and ineffable'.[27] It constitutes the ultimate source of all physical and mental phenomena and the point at which the tensions between fact and value find resolution. Authentic spiritual awareness is a state in which 'the spirit of man "within" is in dialectical harmony with the spirit of the cosmos "beyond".'[28] The truth and meaning of existence are

---

[23] Lealman (1982a): 'The underlying purpose of religious education is to provoke seeing from within a religious perspective, growth within religious awareness. This requires the sharpening of the sense perceptions and the stimulation of the imagination.' p.59.

[24] Priestley (1985).

[25] Starkings (1993a).

[26] Holley (1978), pp.52ff.

[27] ibid., p.61.

[28] ibid., p.59.

not simply the products of human imagination but have a genuine grounding in reality. Our spiritual experience

> intuits that the spiritual order is fundamental to all that exists and that in the spiritual order is to be found the unconditional character of the moral imperative and the power of right action, the inexhaustible depth of genuine creation and the illumination of the beautiful and the lovely, and the desire and longing for embracing the real which is the essence of truth.[29]

Holley distinguishes between this intuition as metaphysical awareness and experience, and any metaphysical explanation of, or speculation about, the natural and rational order.

Holley's framework reflects a general agreement, pervading the mainstream literature, regarding the nature of this spiritual realm.

The nature of the spiritual realm

It is transcendent: spiritual experience places the individual in touch with the 'beyond', the 'other', relating the ordinariness of everyday existence with a higher reality, and allowing one to apprehend 'the strange within the familiar'.[30] Holley sees this in Kantian terms, as the transcending of the world of phenomena and the manifestation of noumenal reality.[31] While some wish to interpret this noumenal realm theologically, others affirm a naturalistic transcendence of human limitations within the immanent structures of time and space.[32]

It is universal: this is seen as supported by empirical evidence for the common occurrence of spiritual experience extending beyond the limiting frameworks of religious traditions.[33] 'We thus can look for the spiritual resources within the entire religious heritage of humankind, but we can equally find pointers to spirituality as transcendence and liberation within

---

[29] Holley (1978), p.53.

[30] Lealman (1982a). '... to experience *myself* within the perspective of transcendence ... and so, to perceive ordinary life in a new way, to see the strange within the familiar,' p.59, italics original; cf. further Lealman (1982b).

[31] Holley, op. cit., pp.46ff.

[32] Contrast Ashraf (1992) and Newby (1994), (1996); cf. Rose (1996).

[33] Grimmit (1987); Hay (1982b); Priestley (1985).

contemporary secular society itself.'[34] Again Hull is a dissenting voice here: approaching spirituality in terms of universal human nature 'tends to undervalue the specific historical and social characteristics of the spirituality which is generated in our society by its present human relationships and practices.'[35]

It is the ground of ultimate value: 'By rooting values in the spiritual givenness of the natural order religion transcends the traditional distinctions of aesthetic, moral and intellectual values over against factual assertions.'[36] Priestley is aware of tensions here and, in distinguishing the 'spiritual child' and the 'child with spirit', suggests that emotive experience is in itself amoral. Consequently he argues that genuine spirituality requires the careful nurturing of the moral dimension.[37]

It is a fundamental mystery: spirituality draws us into a realm in which 'meanings are multi-textured and have many levels of significance: they hover over a multitude of metaphors yet the focus of language slips forever when it seeks to capture them.'[38] Here human understanding is provisional, contingent, elusive and mercurial, possessing the 'quality of something ultimately impenetrable'.[39] For Slee spirituality 'suggests a mystery, an unseen reality, beyond the life of the individual, pervading the entire world order, with which human persons are invited to enter into relationship and communion.'[40]

If the question of the nature of this objective spiritual realm is pursued further – beyond this affirmation of transcendence, universality, value and mystery – a number of different perspectives are encountered. These are fundamentally contradictory and effectively push against the boundaries of the consensus achieved by HMI's anthropological definition.

---

34 King (1985), p.137.

35 Hull (1995b), p.132.

36 Holley (1978), p.53.

37 Priestley (1985).

38 Webster (1982b), p.87.

39 ibid.

40 Slee (1992), p.46.

Theological realism

This takes two forms:

- an affirmation of a diversity of spiritual traditions associated with specific religious communities and belief systems;

- attempts to reconcile these within an all-embracing universal theological framework.[41]

Hay, as we have seen, is quite clear that there are 'grounds for some confidence in the objective reality of the states of awareness achieved in contemplative practice, whatever the variety of interpretations provided by the different traditions.'[42]

Immanent naturalism

Newby, for example, advocates a secular humanistic spirituality that seeks the development of a non-religious faith grounded in human existence itself.[43] It is to be concerned with the discernment of good and evil, the journey towards meaning and purpose, and the liberal search for human well-being. This is to be sharply differentiated from a spirituality grounded in the supernatural realism of orthodox theology. There is, he suggests, 'a shared spirituality abroad in our secular culture ... in which traditional religious belief is superficial or local, and often both.'[44] Further, 'this secular spirituality must not be seen as a rich land to be reclaimed by the church: it is a post-religious spirituality of agapaistic love rising out of the ashes of dead orthodoxy.'[45] He attributes an 'overriding authority [to] our shared framework of secular value commitments'[46] and suggests that

---

[41] For the former cf. e.g. Thatcher (1996): 'Spirituality ... is the practice of the human love of God and neighbour: theology is the study of that practice to enable the followers of Jesus to practise their love of God and their neighbour in informed, direct and appropriate ways', p.119; for the latter cf. e.g. Hay (1985): 'All religious behaviour, without exception, aims to interpret and act upon an experience of the sacred taken at face value', p.141.

[42] Hay (1982a), p.49.

[43] Newby (1994), (1996).

[44] Newby (1994), p.17.

[45] Newby (1994), p.17.

[46] ibid., p.19.

religious education may only be 'deemed educationally successful in so far as it advances spiritual development through secular traditions of knowledge and understanding.'[47]

Post-modern anti-realism

This perspective attempts to pass beyond the realism embodied in both theological supernaturalistic transcendence and secular naturalistic immanence. Erricker, for example, suggests that 'through metaphor we generate meaning and order reality for ourselves in pursuit of mental and spiritual health.'[48] The subject–object duality of modernity, with its desire to affirm objective reality (whether secular or religious) in preference to the subjectivity of the individual, represents a strategy that must be overcome. Metaphorical language is more than mere figurative decoration; it rather constitutes a reality created by inter-subjective communication. 'It is not a matter of distinguishing between religious and non-religious world views nor of determining the ultimate worth of any metaphorical reality but arriving at an appreciation of the metaphorical realities that we all hold.'[49] Here, in an anti-realistic move typical of post-modernism, language becomes the ultimate reality: the question of whether it is capable of depicting an objective world is subservient to the instrumental issue of 'how far ... particular metaphors contribute to or detract from our well-being'.[50] Erricker refers to the iconic quality of mind, the mental imaging that enables us to construct the stories by which we live: 'metaphor actually generates meaning ... it constructs a landscape in which we have a place.'[51] Education should have no concern with objective reality, merely with the pragmatic activity of communicating a rich diversity of metaphorical images. 'Developing communication between and reflecting upon the plurality of our metaphorical perceptions is one of the primary educational tasks that we must address.'[52] Through such an exchange of vision individuals may create for themselves metaphorical

---

[47] ibid., p.19.

[48] Erricker (1993), p. 138; cf. Gearon (1995); Wright (1996c).

[49] Erricker, op. cit., p.144.

[50] ibid., p.138.

[51] ibid., p.139.

[52] Erricker (1993), p.138.

realities that contribute to their physical, mental and spiritual health. 'Learning starts by avoiding the objectification of children and the mythologies of others that we introduce them to ... what we are concerned with here is ... helping children to construct their own enabling metaphors.'[53]

Any attempt to define the spiritual realm beyond the generalised perspective of HMI's anthropological definition thus reveals a fundamental contradiction between theological, naturalistic and post-modern formulations. However, this does not present any fundamental problem for curriculum development. The relationship between spiritual experience and the material content of spiritual insight is as arbitrary, contingent and ultimately unimportant as the relationship of such experience to its cultural forms of expression. What matters is the quality of the experience, not the reality towards which the experience might, or might not, point. Spiritual reality is to be understood in the light of its transcendence, universality, value and mystery: any more detailed definition requires an objectification that undermines the very nature of the spiritual.

It is, on this reading, difficult to ignore a powerful isolationist trend within the discourse of spirituality. The affirmation of the human capacity for spiritual experience entails the rejection of any necessary relationship with both the expression of such experience within culture, and the positive attribution of any material content to the transcendent spiritual realm itself. The relationship between spiritual experience and the true nature of reality is an arbitrary one: in effect the realms of fact and value are polarised. It is not *what* is believed that constitutes an authentic spirituality, but the *means* by which such knowledge is arrived at: the process of attaining spiritual sensibility takes precedence over the material content of spiritual knowledge.

Spiritual Education as the Practice of Freedom

It is, then, possible to identify a contemporary consensus in the educational discourse of spirituality: only a broad liberal understanding of spirituality is appropriate in the contemporary pluralistic educational setting; the spiritual dimension offers a fundamental challenge to the modern objectification of knowledge; narrower theological definitions

---

53 ibid., p.146.

may be accommodated within this liberal perspective provided they are understood as secondary expressions of spiritual experience; insight into the spiritual dimension is a fundamental human capacity; and, finally, its transcendent, universal, value-bearing and mysterious nature is not dependent on any specific world view, whether theological, naturalistic or post-modern.

This consensus has clear implications for educational practice. At its heart spiritual education concerns itself with all those activities 'which sensitise children to the mysteries of life and enable them to view the cosmos, and their place in it, in spiritual terms.'[54] Such sensitisation entails the provoking of a spiritual perspective, leading to depth of insight through 'the sharpening of the sense perceptions and the stimulation of the imagination'.[55] This 'training in sensitivity for spiritual awareness'[56] must 'begin and end with pupils' own inwardness'[57] by providing them with access to their own 'inner space'. 'The great purpose of education should be to give people a greater reliance on the validity of their own inward and private experience.'[58]

This starting-point rejects the limitations of modernity. The role of education is to liberate pupils from secular metaphor and 'the taboos which inhibit them from exploring freely the experiential and cognitive options available'.[59] This task of combating secular consciousness is distinct from the illegitimate confessional task of 'reasserting the viability if not the necessity of religious belief'.[60] It entails a fundamental shift in the aims of education: the traditionalist concern for the transmission of knowledge is replaced by the progressive commitment to the development of the whole child's well-being. 'To attempt to educate the spirit is to attempt to affect what a person is and what he or she might become, not

---

[54] Holley, op. cit., p.65.

[55] Lealman (1982a), p.59.

[56] King (1985), p.138.

[57] Priestley (1985), p.118.

[58] Priestley (1992), p.35.

[59] Hay (1985), p.146.

[60] Grimmitt (1987): 'Such a view ... comes close to making religious education an instrument of religious ideology', p.136.

just what they can do or might know.'[61] For Slee personal education as method, process and exploration has priority over academic education as content, programme and instruction.[62]

Learning is an artistic process sculptured by teachers who themselves 'are on the endless road of spiritual search.'[63] Both teachers and pupils bring their whole selves to this creative process as personal resource centres. The teacher must 'dare to realise his own creativity, blacken his fingers with charcoal.'[64] Only then can a genuine, imaginative and creative learning process come into being. Such a process, like spirituality itself, crosses all boundaries. Spiritual education is the concern of the whole curriculum: school ethos, relationships between staff, pupils and parents and the broader community, the pastoral system, collective worship, cross-curricular themes, and all the specific subject disciplines. To plan this process too tightly runs the risk of suffocating it, while the option of passively waiting for spirituality to manifest itself spontaneously invites failure.

Spiritual education demands the sharpening of children's perceptual awareness of the physical world. There is a place in the classroom 'for branches and roots – twisting, curling; for bark with rough deep texture; for pebbles for touching and holding.'[65] It entails the stimulation of the pupils' sense of awe and wonder through a process that, for Webster, entails re-focusing understanding at greater depths; introducing new facets of common objects; provoking insight through symbols; valuing self-questioning; observing the element of mystery within reason and explanation; keeping alive the intensity of childhood experience; provoking nonconformity and insight.[66] It must provide triggers for the imagination,[67] access to images to be appropriated, broken and

---

61 Priestley (1985), p.115.

62 Slee (1992).

63 Priestley, op. cit., p.119.

64 Lealman (1982a), p.62.

65 ibid., p.60.

66 Webster (1982a).

67 Lealman (1982a), p.61.

recreated,[68] and awareness of the boundary situations of the human condition.[69] Of all the subject areas within the curriculum, such processes have their closest affinity with the creative arts, since 'the essential function of art is to stimulate the imagination, to set it free.'[70]

Spiritual education has to do with 'a new innocence of perception'[71] through which 'the mystery is disclosed – [since] it can never be taught.'[72] The role of the knowledge contained within the various subject disciplines thus becomes an extrinsic one. The language, symbols and cultural objects that form the heart of the various subject disciplines within the curriculum are studied for the sake of spiritual insight, not for knowledge and understanding. They have value not in themselves but instrumentally as the means of stimulating spiritual experience. Language is ultimately transcended. Attempts to demonstrate convergence between experience and its expressions[73] seek to illuminate the experience rather than explore the expression. An education concerned with concepts and the intellect must understand its role as that of servant of an education focused on feelings and experience. 'Teachers proceed from practice to interpretation by giving their pupils a scientific language and concepts which will enable them to enter more deeply and subtly into their experience.'[74] The extent of this anti-intellectualism appears most strongly in Priestley's suggestion that though the intellect must not be neglected – since '*for those who are capable*, scaling the mountains of academic achievement provides as much spiritual exhilaration as the conquest of literal mountains does for the physically robust'[75] – nevertheless 'our failure lies in trying to make everyone climb the same mountains.'[76]

---

[68] Lealman (1982b).

[69] Webster, op. cit.

[70] Robinson (1982), p.52.

[71] Lealman (1982a), p.62.

[72] ibid.

[73] e.g. Webster (1985).

[74] Hay (1985), p.144.

[75] Priestley (1985), p.119, my italics.

[76] ibid.

The process and function of spiritual education are thus clearly linked with the theoretical perspectives outlined here. The insights of Religious Education are universalised as the discourse of spiritual education adopts a cross-curricular perspective: the spiritual dimension is an essential aspect of human nature, and authentic spirituality is equated with an experiential capacity sensitive to the dimensions of transcendence, universality, value and mystery inherent within human spirituality. Questions of the material content of spiritual insight, knowledge and truth are secondary to the primary concern for the development of spiritual sensibility; as a result, spiritual education is concerned with the development of the capacity for spiritual sensibility, one effectively dislocated from any positive material content.

Together these concepts offer a coherent and highly influential educational vision. The task of the second part of this study is to investigate the roots of this consensus further and so explore its viability and authenticity.

Part Two

Critique:

Flaws in the Consensus

4. The Romantic/Post-modern Tradition

The approach to spirituality outlined in Part One revealed a remarkably consistent theoretical framework and practical programme. It claims to have unveiled the universal anthropological and epistemological structures of spirituality previously hidden by the excesses of modernity. Part Two of this study offers a critique of this assertion of the comprehensive efficacy of the current consensus.

The Spiritual Dilemma of Modernity

Modernity proclaims itself as the age of the triumph of reason and emancipation from superstition.[1] However, the recognition of flaws in the modernist programme has resulted in reason itself being understood as an instrument of constraint. Unbridled rationalism can be pathological, undermining authentic human freedom. Both the romantic and post-modern critiques of modernism seek to escape from this tyranny of rationality: one by asserting the primary importance of feeling over reason, the other by deconstructing all forms of rational thought.[2] The contemporary discourse of spirituality shares the belief of these critiques that they recover a primordial dimension of human awareness and freedom otherwise eclipsed by modernity.

Despite the attractiveness of this scenario it is not without its difficulties. Both romanticism and post-modernism operate within the structures of

---

[1] For the history of the roots of modernity in the Enlightenment cf. Buckley (1987); Cassirer (1951); Gay (1973a), (1973b); for the present philosophical critique of modernity cf. Adorno & Horkheimer (1972); Bernstein (1983); Foucault (1989), (1991); Gadamer (1979); Gellner (1992); Habermas (1987a), (1987b), (1987c), (1987d); MacIntyre (1985), (1988); Maxwell (1987); Polanyi (1958); Ricoeur (1974), (1977); Rorty (1980); Taylor (1992); Wright (1995).

[2] For the romantic critique of rationalism cf. note 1, above; the classic attack on romanticism remains Nietzsche (1986); cf. Kaufmann (1974), pp.3–18.

modernity, and offer not the recovery of an authentic dimension of reality, but merely a mirror-image of modernism.[3] Both the romantic affirmation of feeling over reason, and the post-modern rejection of rationality, take the Enlightenment's celebration of the intellect as their starting point. By defining themselves against modernity, romanticism and post-modernity allow that tradition a formative authority. They are thus ultimately dependent upon, and hence reflect the flaws of the very culture they seek to undermine. As a result the accounts of spirituality within the romantic and post-modern paradigms, rather than having universal significance, reflect a particular spiritual tradition rooted in late twentieth-century Western culture's response to the fragmentation of the narratives of modernity.

At the heart of modernity stands Descartes' attempt to establish knowledge that is certain.[4] His concern is to escape from that which Bernstein describes as 'Cartesian anxiety': the fear that reality is essentially meaningless.[5] The dilemma confronting Descartes is clear: 'either there is some support for our being, a fixed foundation for our knowledge, or we cannot escape the forces of darkness that envelop us with madness, with intellectual and moral chaos.'[6] If knowledge is to be sure, then its foundations must be stable. The path to understanding entails a hermeneutic of suspicion: the received authority of tradition, the legitimacy of perceptions of the external world, and the integrity of mental constructs are all subjected to the crucible of a radical scepticism. Only by thus stripping away illusion, error and falsehood is it possible to establish legitimate knowledge on a secure basis.

This hermeneutic of suspicion produces an individualistic anthropology that effectively dislocates the self from its cultural and historical context, from any authentic relationship with the external reality of the natural order, and from association with other selves in community.[7] It is this image of selfhood as essentially isolated, dislocated and autonomous that has dominated modern thought. It is not awareness of one's place in the

---

3 Gadamer (1979), pp.172ff, 242ff.

4 Descartes (1970).

5 cf. Bernstein (1983), pp.16–20.

6 ibid., p.18.

7 cf. Taylor (1992); McFadyen (1990); Wright (1996b); Yu (1987).

world and one's relationship with others that constitutes authentic selfhood, but inner reflection, contemplation and self-understanding. The modern ideal is of self-sufficiency and emancipation from external constraint.

The discovery of authentic knowledge is dependent on the ability of the dislocated mind to avoid illusion by accurately mirroring reality in its consciousness.[8] Here modernity operates with two basic criteria for truth: the convergence of thought and language with external reality, and the internal coherence of ideas. The former appears in the empirical tradition that understands truth as the sum of verifiable statements concerning the natural world. The latter operates in the idealistic tradition that understands truth as the ability of the mind to construct a coherent and all-embracing system of rational knowledge. Fundamental to modernity is the belief that, whatever the adopted criteria, the mind can indeed achieve knowledge of the order and nature of reality.

Both romantic and post-modern critiques suggest that the flaws inherent in modernity are rooted in the tendency of both empiricism and idealism to become repressive instruments that constrain human freedom.

Empiricism reduces reality to the brute facts of the natural world. The physical order, conditioned by the inevitability of the ongoing flow of cause and effect, takes on a deterministic nature. This reduces human beings to the level of natural animals constrained and controlled by their physical natures. The domain of fact is separated from, and given authority over, that of value. Questions of human worth and freedom, of our ability to participate authentically in the spheres of religion, morality and aesthetics, are relativised. Affirmations of transcendence, goodness and beauty become optional beliefs, mere opinions rather than genuine claims to knowledge. This leads to a further diminution of human freedom: technological progress, driven by scientific possibility divorced from any considerations of value, produces military and industrial machinery that threatens both the human and environmental good.[9]

Idealism also becomes a source of constraint, due ultimately to its inability to distinguish authentic knowledge from mere speculation. If idealistic truth is dependent on the inner coherence of its ideas alone, then it is possible to regard any system as legitimate provided it possesses an

---

[8] Rorty (1980).

[9] Adorno & Horkheimer (1972).

internal unity. There is nothing to stop such schemes from springing out of a rich subjective imagination that has no connection with reality. Treating such speculative knowledge as possessing universal validity and applying it in practical political contexts risks creating an authoritarian instrument of repression. Here idealised speculation represents the pseudo-science of a closed society. If the internal coherence of an idealised system is not open to external scrutiny it develops 'a charmed circle of unchanging taboos, of laws and customs which are felt to be as inevitable as the rising of the sun, or the cycle of the seasons.'[10] Fascism and Marxism are classic examples of idealised systems grounded in mythical ideologies that violently curtail human freedom.

Given these authoritarian tendencies, modernity faces the urgent practical need to protect the autonomy of the individual. Liberalism achieves this by distinguishing objective public knowledge from subjective private belief, and by asserting the absolute freedom of the individual as regards the latter.[11] The only limit to such freedom is the demand that we are willing to tolerate the beliefs of others. This leads to Popper's paradox of tolerance: 'we should claim, in the name of tolerance, the right not to tolerate the intolerant.'[12] Consequently beliefs and values become optional extras: the individual is free to adopt any set of beliefs she or he chooses, guided only by personal preference and inclination. Religious, aesthetic and moral truths are thus relativised and privatised, divorced from any necessary relationship with external reality.

Modern rationalism, despite its promise to provide emancipation and enlightenment, unleashes forces of constraint and superstition. Romanticism and post-modernism are at the forefront of this critique of modernity, though we have already seen that these twin movements depend upon modernity while opposing it. In affirming the failure of the modern trust in reason, romanticism and post-modernism draw on and develop a number of other themes inherent within modernity itself: the image of the dislocated self, the division of fact and value, and the understanding as freedom as emancipation from constraint. Thus modernity and its romantic / post-modern critique represent two sides of the same coin.

---

[10] Popper (1966), p.57.

[11] This tradition can be traced from Popper back to John Locke.

[12] Popper, op. cit., p.265.

The Romantic Critique of Modernity

The romantic critique of the legacy of the Enlightenment flourished in the late eighteenth and early nineteenth centuries. Romanticism was a broad-ranging cultural and intellectual movement that embraced art, literature, poetry, music and philosophy.[13] Its religious dimension, associated above all with Schleiermacher and the tradition of liberal Protestant theology, is considered in the next chapter.[14] Though romanticism as a concrete movement faded relatively quickly, its legacy continues to pervade contemporary thought.[15] It is suggested below that post-modernism represents a radical extension of the romantic tradition.

Romanticism springs directly from a critique of the limitations of modern culture. For Rousseau, the repressive nature of culture is confirmation that 'everything is good as it comes from the hands of the maker of things; everything degenerates in the hands of man.'[16] The new age promised by the Enlightenment has deteriorated into a civilisation dominated by a rationality that stifles the human spirit. It is in the domain of the arts that this failure of reason is most transparent. Romanticism rejects the classical aesthetic of the Enlightenment that demands that art 'be measured and tested by the rules of reason'[17]. In the classical tradition it is the form of the work of art that is all-important, and the genuine artist conforms to the traditional rules governing artistic style. 'Classicism is an eminently logical system, which scorns the waywardness of unschooled genius, values reason above imagination and knowledge above persons.'[18] Such a restrictive art mirrors the order and structure of modern life that, once dominated by reason, quickly becomes arid and sterile.

---

[13] The pantheon of romantic 'geniuses' includes: Beethoven, Byron, Coleridge, Diderot, Goethe, Hazlitt, Herder, Keats, Lessing, Novalis, Rousseau, A.W. Schlegel, F. von Schlegel, Shelly and Wordsworth.

[14] cf. Reardon (1985).

[15] Kermode (1971).

[16] Rousseau (1986), p.56, following the translation of Bowen (1981) p.187; cf. above, chapter 1, note 23.

[17] Cassirer (1951), p.279.

[18] Chambers (1932), p.80.

Kermode sees the alternative to rationalism as the recovery of the 'romantic image'.[19] It is the apprehension and epiphany of 'the Image as a radiant truth out of space and time'[20] that dominates the romantic sensibility. This romantic vision transcends the mediocrity inherent in the academic and dogmatic neo-classical affirmation of reason. In its place it affirms the dynamic effervescence and vitality of human feeling, empathy, emotion and spiritual sensitivity. The romantics were able to 'discover heights and depths of the human spirit that the older philosophy had hardly dared dream of.'[21] For Rousseau's romanticism it is the recovery of natural reason that returns the individual to an uncorrupted relationship with the natural order. He seeks a recovery of 'the superior wisdom of the primeval age of myth'.[22] Such wisdom affirms the superiority of feeling over rationality, intuitive insight over cognitive certainty: 'the more I strive ... the less do I comprehend ... the less I understand, the more I adore. I feel it, experience it.'[23] The romantic sensibility thus uncovers the possibility of a depth and breadth of human experience that transcends the ordinary and mundane.

If romanticism rejected modernism's rationality, it held fast to its image of the dislocated self. The achievement of the romantic vision is the task of the isolated genius. The true romantic artist is free to break the formal rules of art, and possesses the courage to pursue his or her vision in the spiritual quest for the romantic image.[24] Kermode draws attention to the

---

[19] Kermode (1971).

[20] ibid., p.30.

[21] Chambers (1932), p.163.

[22] Gadamer (1979), p.243.

[23] Rousseau (1986), p.249.

[24] Perhaps the classic example of this myth of artistic genius is found in the romantic reading of the life and work of Beethoven. In his final chamber and instrumental works, composed in an isolation from society exacerbated by deafness, he moves beyond traditional classical musical forms, exploring the potential of the fugue, theme and variation in a style that constantly refers back on itself in a process of ever deeper introspection. The romantic tension between joy and despair, loss and fulfilment, is reflected in the contrast between the simplicity of melody and dissonance of harmony that is produced. The genius of the music reflects the genius of the man, both being rooted in isolation and suffering. This myth had already taken hold at the time of his death. The funeral oration, written

romantic myth that it is only in 'the necessary isolation or estrangement of men' that the romantic sensibility is perfected;[25] the artist 'has to pay a heavy price in suffering, to risk his immortal soul, and to be alone.'[26] It is the artist's vocation to look inwards, to experience with a depth of insight and intensity not available to ordinary mortals, to glimpse a vision of the divine realm that transcends the mundane world of everyday life, and then bring such experience to expression in artistic works of genius.

The combination of the romantic image and romantic notion of the artist as creative genius perpetuates a further theme within modernity, that of the dualism of fact and value. The romantic vision, by turning inwards, passes beyond the natural world into a transcendent realm. The combination of subjectivity and truth reinforces the modernist distinction between objective reality and subjective experience. As Cassirer points out 'sentiment is always right ... has a reference to nothing beyond itself, and is always real, whenever a man is conscious of it.'[27]

Kant provides a philosophical framework within which this romantic critique of modernity developed.[28] Proceeding from the image of the dislocated self he distinguishes phenomenal from noumenal reality. The phenomenological world is the reality of things as they appear to us, filtered through our perceptions within the fixed framework of time, space

---

by Grillparzer and spoken by Anschutz, already understands him as a man of genius, set apart from ordinary mortals: 'He was an artist, but a man as well ... He fled the world because, in the whole range of his loving nature, he found no weapon to oppose it. He withdrew from mankind after he had given them his all and received nothing in return', Sonneck (1954), p.230. Dahlhaus (1993), in the process of deconstructing this romantic myth, outlines its basic structure: 'Yet even if subjectivity is not always or necessarily implied by musical expressivity, it is all the more marked as a characteristic of the music of Beethoven ... ..His work is perceived as 'subjective' to a degree that was unknown to earlier generations. The literature about Beethoven is the prime example of writing where the emotional elements that are adjunct to the 'musical object', the imagined 'aesthetic subject' whose expression they appear to be, and the empirical person of the composer, as reconstructed from the biographical documentation, mingle almost inseparably.' p.31.

[25] Kermode (1971), p.13.

[26] ibid.

[27] Cassirer (1951), p.318.

[28] Kant (1934); cf. Fackenheim (1985); Walsh (1967).

and the categories of our understanding. The noumenal world is the realm of things as they are in themselves. This is the realm of ultimate reality, of God, beauty and goodness, transcending the deterministic phenomenological reality of our everyday perceptions. We have no direct access to this transcendent dimension through the exercise of our reason, yet we are still capable of intimating it. 'Noumenal reality is disclosed to us, not through reason itself, but through humankind's experience.'[29] Through the practical obligations of the categorical imperative, that we treat others as ends in themselves, the noumenal world is revealed intuitively to us. From the categorical imperative Kant moves outward to invoke the immortality of the soul, God, human freedom and a transcendent ground for aesthetic judgements of taste. Such noumenal knowledge is not arrived at through reason and deduction, but is rather grounded in the practical need to live within the phenomenal world as if under the shadow of transcendence, eternity and the numinous.

The romantic movement adopts and develops the programme of Kant. In a self-conscious contrast with modernity it upholds the values of feeling, immediate apprehension and artistic creativity over those of reason, critical reflection and scientific discovery. It sees in empiricism and idealism structures that serve to constrain human freedom, and so seeks emancipation from them. Freedom from the tyranny of the phenomenal world is achieved through the observation that our phenomenological knowledge is not absolute, but relative to the limitations of our perceptions. As such, it provides access not to the world as it actually is, merely to the world as it appears to us. Such knowledge is thus contingent and as such has no absolute constraining power over us. Authentic human freedom is grounded in the possibility of experience and feeling directed towards the noumenal realm of reality as it is in itself, that dimension of ultimate truth, beauty and goodness which we cannot know rationally, but which we can nevertheless intuit through our religious, artistic and moral sensibilities.

The parallels between this romantic programme and the contemporary discourse of spirituality are transparent. In each modernity is viewed with suspicion; natural and cultural phenomena are dismissed as lacking any inherent value; and the primary task of humanity is affirmed as being that of transcending the limitations of the phenomenal world in favour of a primal and unconstrained intuition of transcendent noumenal reality.

---

[29] Fackenheim (1985), p.29.

However, despite this, romanticism remains dependent upon modernity: there is an identical starting-point in the image of the dislocated self; the romantic categories are developed in polar opposition to modernity; and the fact–value distinction remains firmly in place. Gadamer points out that, as such, romanticism offers a mirror image of modernity: 'the romantic reversal of this [rationalistic] criterion of the Enlightenment actually perpetuates the abstract contrast between myth and reason.'[30] Not only is romanticism dependent upon modernity, it also paves the way for post-modern perspectives. For Torrance the polarity between phenomenal fact and noumenal value 'had the effect of giving rise to a romantic idealism where the human spirit could range at will, uncontrolled by scientific evidence or knowledge.'[31] Post-modernity may be seen as the radicalisation of this romantic assertion of the freedom of the human spirit from any external constraint.

From Romanticism to Post-modernity

Post-modernity proceeds from the same moral imperative present at the heart of both modernity and romanticism: the drive towards emancipation and freedom.[32] As Taylor asserts, the post-modern tradition 'reflects that the underlying ideal is some variant of that most invisible, because it is the most pervasive, of all modern goods, unconstrained freedom.'[33] It seeks freedom not merely from pre-modern superstition, but also from the constraints of modernity's empirical and idealistic discourses, and further, from romanticism's assertion of the transcendent intuition of ultimate reality. Foucault thus rejects the belief that the resources for the construction of a lasting picture of reality and human nature are to be found in the immediate self-consciousness of the dislocated self. The modern and romantic images of humanity have no essential substance and will inevitably be erased 'like a face drawn in sand at the edge of the

---

30 Gadamer (1979), p.243.

31 Torrance (1980), p.25.

32 On post-modernity, cf. Bauman (1994); Boyne (1990); Foucault (1989), (1991); Gasche (1986); Lyotard (1984); Norris (1987), (1993); Rorty (1980), (1989); Sarup (1988).

33 Taylor (1992), p.489.

sea'.[34] The entire intellectual history of the liberal West is dismissed as 'a momentary "fold" in the fabric of knowledge'.[35]

The task of post-modernity is two-fold. First, there is the establishment of absolute freedom through the deconstruction of any system of thought or truth claim that denies the contingency and relativity of human knowledge. For Derrida all such traditions must be challenged, but they can be challenged only internally.[36] There is no transcendent vantage point from which the post-modern philosopher can operate. We are immersed in a series of local linguistic traditions and there is no possibility of finding 'a meta-vocabulary which somehow takes account of all possible vocabularies'.[37] The task of post-modernism is thus the ongoing process of the establishment of autonomy through the continuous deconstruction of inherited cultural traditions. We cannot escape these traditions, but we can establish our freedom within them by cultivating the habit of irony through which we learn not to treat them with any degree of seriousness.

Secondly, post-modernity demands the practice of freedom through the celebration of our ability to utilise language and culture in the ongoing game of constructing, deconstructing and reconstructing images of reality on the grounds of personal desire, inclination and preference. Rorty, following Gadamer, sees this as a process of 'substituting the notion of Bildung (education, self-formation) for that of knowledge as the goal of thinking.'[38] There is no ultimate reality within post-modernity, merely the celebration of our freedom to construct our own personal and necessarily disposable world-views.

> To keep a conversation going is a sufficient aim of philosophy, to see wisdom as consisting in the ability to sustain a conversation, is to see human beings as generators of new descriptions ... More important, it would regard the realisation of utopias, and the envisaging of still further utopias, as an endless process − an endless, proliferating

---

[34] Foucault (1989), p.387.

[35] Norris (1987), p.221.

[36] Derrida (1976), (1978), (1982).

[37] Rorty (1989), p.xvi.

[38] Rorty (1980), p.359.

realisation of freedom, rather than a convergence toward an already existing truth.[39]

Once again the relationship of post-modernity with the contemporary discourse of spirituality is opaque. The romantic shift from reason to feeling is radicalised in the affirmation that the authenticity of such feeling is grounded not in its relationship with any transcendent reality but in the autonomous decision of the individual to utilise a particular cultural heritage instrumentally as a provider of the building blocks necessary for the game of personal reality creation. Spirituality, within an educational context, has travelled the same route. At heart, contemporary spiritual education has embarked on a process of inducting pupils into the rules of the post-modern game, encouraging them to construct their own realities on the basis of unrestrained freedom, desire, will and preference.

However, it is a false move to see this as a universal inevitability, forced upon us by the collapse of both modernity and romanticism. The fragmentation of modernity has given birth to alternative traditions of critical realism that set themselves against both modernity and post-modernism. There is nothing given, universal or inevitable about the post-modern interpretation of the human condition. It merely constitutes that particular tradition which sets out to deconstruct all traditions, that specific assertion of the truth that there is no truth. Like romantic spirituality before it, post-modern spirituality reflects an identifiable tradition that embodies a given reading of the nature of reality and of the spiritual structures that flow from its positive assertions. The continuity between the two allows us to speak of a romantic / post-modern spiritual tradition, one whose truth claims must be read in relationship to the truth claims of alternative spiritual traditions.

It has been suggested in this chapter that, far from uncovering a universal dimension of human spiritual potential, the contemporary educational discourse must be read as rooted in provincial attempts within the modern Western intellectual tradition to escape the excesses of modernity. It does this by identifying and challenging the authoritarian rationalism of the modern idealistic and empirical traditions, and by supplementing them with a romantic critique. It further rejects an authoritarian influence within romanticism itself by asserting the post-modern belief that romantic sensibility must be reduced to a series of relativistic cultural games, ones always localised and dependent upon the individual freedom to construct

---

[39] Rorty (1980), p.378.

perceptions of reality at will, unconstrained by any universal claims implied by the romantic tradition.

5. Trinitarian Christian Spirituality

The previous chapter suggested that the contemporary discourse of spirituality is not universal, but dependent on a parochial romantic / post-modern tradition of reaction against modernity. This may be reinforced by contrasting romantic spirituality with the spirituality of Christian Trinitarian orthodoxy. If Christian spirituality, in its historical continuity, is incompatible with romantic and post-modern formulations, then the latter can claim universality only by deconstructing orthodox Christian discourse and colonising it within its own frame of reference. Consequently universality can be affirmed only through a special pleading that does violence to alternative spiritual traditions.

The Challenge of Liberal Theology

The Enlightenment's hermeneutic of suspicion directed towards received cultural traditions effectively undermined the reliance of orthodox Christianity on revelation within history, authoritatively transmitted through scripture and the teaching office of the church.[1] It attempted to replace revelation with forms of natural theology, circumnavigating the claims of revealed theology and attempting to ground knowledge of God on human reason alone; these attempts failed when seen in the light of the historical continuity of the Christian faith. On the one hand, the rational arguments for such a natural theology were deemed inadequate; on the other, the deistic God that emerged was clearly incompatible with the Trinitarian God of Christian orthodoxy.[2] This led to a polarisation between the atheistic rejection of religious belief and the affirmation of faith. Forced on the defensive, Christianity increasingly sought justification in the absolute authority of either church or scripture. Such a strategy

---

[1] Bartley (1964); Buckley (1987); Jungel (1983); Kung (1980).

[2] Hume (1947); Pascal (1966).

produced forms of fideism and fundamentalism that lacked any syncronicity with the structures of modernity.

Beginning from Schleiermacher, liberal theology attempted an accommodation between faith and modern culture by drawing on the resources of romanticism.[3] The romantic intuition of transcendence provided an alternative ground for faith to that of revelation authenticated by the authority of church and scripture. Religious doctrines constituted not descriptions of reality in conflict with the world-view of modern science, but rather expressions of inner religious experience.[4] For Schleiermacher the experience of being absolutely dependent is at the same time experience of God.[5] This enabled faith to find a home within the modern world, but only at the expense of introducing a division between religious language and reality: religious doctrines now referred primarily to subjective religious sensibility and had only a secondary and contingent relationship with objective reality. As a result Christian liberalism slipped easily into forms of universal theology.[6] Rather than Christian doctrine being the only authentic expression of religious experience, it became possible to understand all religious traditions as culturally determined and equally valid expressions of a common religious experience. It was no longer important if the doctrinal systems of different world faiths were in conflict with one another, since what mattered was not the reality they described but the experience they expressed. Religious traditions took their place within a romantic framework in which numinous reality is first glimpsed through primary pre-linguistic experience and then verbalised as second-order religious expression.

The passage from romanticism to its radicalisation in post-modernism is reflected in the development of this experiential–expressive model of

---

[3] Schleiermacher (1958), (1976); cf. Avis (1986) pp.1–23.

[4] Lindbeck (1984).

[5] cf. Schleiermacher (1976): 'The piety which forms the basis of all ecclesiastical communions is ... neither a knowing nor a Doing, but a modification of Feeling, or of immediate self-consciousness ... the self-identical essence of piety is this: the consciousness of being absolutely dependent, or, which is the same thing, of being in relation with God ... Christian Doctrines are accounts of the Christian religious affections set forth in speech,' pp.5, 12, 76.

[6] Hick (1977), (1989); Smith (1978); cf. D' Costa (1990); Hick & Knitter (1987).

religious language.[7] The post-modern critique of romanticism denies the reality of any transcendent realm, claiming that nothing can be postulated beyond the immanent artefacts of cultural tradition. Radical theological liberalism, in advocating anti-realistic forms of theological discourse and deconstructing traditions of theological realism, simply follows in the footsteps of post-modernism's interpretation of romanticism. Post-modern forms of negative and anti-realistic theology understand religious language neither as descriptive of reality, nor as expressive of transcendent experience, but as a practical resource through which the autonomous individual may, if so inclined, construct a model of reality that conforms to her or his own private desires and needs. This reduction of religious traditions to the level of mere utility is, as has been seen, a theme central to the contemporary discourse of spirituality within education.

The path from modernity through romanticism into post-modernity is thus a path from certainty into agnosticism. The dislocated self attempts to use reason to establish a relationship with external reality, turning to emotion when reason fails, and ultimately recognising that there can be no access to any reality beyond the one we create for ourselves. If Descartes saw this fundamental isolation of the human self as a source of anxiety, Derrida sees it as something to be celebrated. The human spirit joins in this celebration, rejoicing in its emancipation from the constraints of religious dogma, retaining an emotive hold on a transcendent sensibility, and ultimately relinquishing even that in favour of a spirituality of absolute individual autonomy and freedom that is fundamentally agnostic about any reality other that of the dislocated self. In this process the truth claims of Christian orthodoxy are fundamentally undermined: Christian doctrine is at best a relativistic expression of a universal experience, at worst a fiction that may be utilised as a building block in the post-modern cyclical game of reality construction, deconstruction and reconstruction.

The Foundations of Christian Spirituality

Christian theology starts from a hermeneutic not of suspicion but of trust.[8] Authentic freedom lies not in emancipation from the constraints of reality,

---

[7] Berry & Wernick (1992); Coward & Foshay (1992); Cupitt (1987), (1991); Handelmann (1982); Hart (1991); Liechty (1990); Taylor (1982), (1984).

[8] For orthodox theological critiques of the romantic/post-modern tradition of liberal theology cf. Gunton (1985), (1993); Ingraffia (1995); Jungel (1983); Kerr (1986); Louth (1989); Middleton & Walsh (1995); Milbank (1993); Moltmann

but in authentic relationship with God and his creation. True rationality lies not in any abstracted, reified and autonomous reason, but in understanding that accommodates itself to the objective claims of the actuality of divine revelation. Authentic faith is rooted not in self-reflection leading to an unmediated experience of a Unitarian God, but in a relationship with the Trinitarian God dependent on the mediation of revelation through scripture and ecclesiastical tradition.[9] True knowledge is grounded in faith's seeking understanding of the divine reality that transcends and stands over against humanity. The reality that God is always one step beyond human comprehension demands the affirmation of contingent rationality rather than a descent into agnosticism. The doctrine of the Trinity is not a culturally relative expression of the subjective religious experience of Christians, but an objective description of divine reality whose source is not human sensibility but divine revelation. This Christian orthodoxy clearly contradicts the structures of modernity, romanticism and post-modernity, and its inner integrity demands not an attempt at accommodation within modernist structures but a critique of modernity in the light of Christian truth.

Christianity accepts the possibility of natural knowledge of God. However, unlike romanticism, such knowledge is not grounded in the eclipse of the natural world and human rationality. It is precisely through the aesthetic appreciation and scientific investigation of his creation that God is revealed.[10] The romantic distrust of the objective and potentially repressive nature of natural science is thus clearly challenged by Christian theology. The Christian God is known through the objectivity of his immanent creation rather than in any subjective transcendence of physical reality. Natural theology proceeds not by denying the natural world and seeking dislocation from it, but by affirming it and seeking proper relationship within it.

(1974); Newbigin (1986); Pannenberg (1976); Paul (1987); Peukert (1986); Thompson (1990); Torrance (1962), (1965), (1969), (1980); Tracey (1981); Yu (1987).

[9] Christian orthodoxy is understood in terms of the historical continuity of Trinitarian doctrine; cf. Gunton (1991); Jungel (1976).

[10] Barbour (1968); Jaki (1978); Peacocke (1971), (1984), (1993); Polkinghorne (1986), (1988).

Such natural knowledge of God is immediately qualified within the Christian tradition.[11] The doctrine of original sin fundamentally limits the human capacity to know God through the light of reason. If appropriated apart from specific revelation, our natural knowledge of God falls inevitably into idolatry. As a result, humanity either lacks the capacity altogether to distinguish God from his creation, or at best is able to perceive God behind creation only hesitantly and fleetingly. Thus Calvin argues that the distance between God and humanity, already great, is further increased by sin.[12] Once again the foundation of Christian spirituality must be distinguished from that advocated by the romantic / post-modern tradition. Rousseau's denial of original sin, his affirmation of the natural goodness of humanity and reliance on the ultimate authenticity of immediate experience constitutes a form of neo-Pelagianism incompatible with Christian teaching.

It is this distinction between the original innocence of humanity and our fallen nature that provides the focal point of the Christian understanding of spirituality. This theological dualism is to be contrasted with the metaphysical and epistemological dualisms within the romantic / post-modern tradition. The modernist distinctions between body and soul, physical and spiritual, fact and value, object and subject and immanence and transcendence are not part of Christian teaching. Rather, Christianity affirms a theological contrast, between a spiritual life of authentic relationship with God, and a fleshly life – understood not as physical existence but as the existence of humanity under the influence of the Fall – in which such a relationship is disrupted.

> Those who are living by their natural inclinations have their minds on the things human nature desires; those who live in the spirit have their minds on spiritual things. And human nature has nothing to look forward to but death, while the spirit looks forward to life and peace, because the outlook of disordered human nature is opposed to God ... when Christ is in you, the body is dead because of sin but the spirit is alive because you have been justified.[13]

---

[11] The nature of this qualification varies within the broad Trinitarian tradition; the most thoroughgoing is that of Karl Barth. Barth & Brunner (1946).

[12] Calvin (1960), pp.43–50.

[13] Romans 8:5–7, 10.

This Pauline distinction between flesh and spirit is concerned with the question 'whether one tries to establish truth and righteousness on one's own or whether one relies upon the Spirit of God for salvation.'[14] The flawed foundation of romantic / post-modern spirituality lies in its trust in human nature, which can lead only to the idolatry of human desire. Christian spirituality has its source not in human nature but in the Spirit of God.

The Source of Christian Spirituality

Christian spirituality has its source in the Holy Spirit, the third person of the Trinity, consubstantial with the Father and the Son, who 'with the Father and the Son ... is worshipped and glorified.'[15] As God's *ruach* – breath, wind, spirit – the Spirit is the power of God through whom his redemptive purpose for creation is achieved. 'The Holy Spirit is at work with the Father and the Son from the beginning to the completion of the plan for our salvation.'[16] The affirmations of the creeds give a systematic formulation to a realistic narrative story grounded in the objectivity of the divine reality and of God's providential plan for humanity through creation, redemption and reconciliation.

'Yahweh God shaped man from the soil of the ground and blew the breath of life into his nostrils, and man became a living being.'[17] It is from the Spirit of God that the human spirit derives, and upon whom life is dependent. 'Take back their breath and they die and revert to dust. Send out your breath and life begins.'[18] As well as being the giver and sustainer of life, the Spirit is also the instrument of God's actions in history. The classical prophets are chosen, called and set apart to speak God's word by the Spirit, experiencing not a moment of romantic self-illumination but the interruption of divine reality within fallen nature. Their eschatological message, of the future outpouring of God's Spirit on all the earth, is linked to Messianic expectations:

---

14 Ingraffia (1995) p.202.

15 The Nicene Creed; cf. Catechism (1994), Kelly (1950) pp.205–230.

16 Catechism, op. cit., p.158.

17 Genesis 2:7.

18 Psalm 104 :29f.

There shall come forth a shoot from the stump of Jesse,
and a branch shall grow out of his roots.
And the Spirit of the LORD shall rest upon him,
the spirit of wisdom and understanding,
the spirit of counsel and might,
the spirit of knowledge and the fear of the LORD.[19]

The dawning of the new age of the Spirit, in which the fullness of life is poured out for all, not merely upon God's chosen prophets and messengers, comes with the incarnation. Through the Spirit Mary conceives; through the Spirit Jesus heals, teaches and goes to the cross; through the Spirit Christ achieves atonement, the redemption of fallen humanity, and the reconciliation of fallen creation to its creator.

Authentic life, the life lived in proper relationship with God, is possible through the outpouring of the Holy Spirit at Pentecost. It is here that the first-fruits of the new age are grasped. By living in the Spirit, received at baptism, the Christian can realise the fruit of the Spirit: 'love, joy, peace, patience, kindness, goodness, faithfulness, gentleness, self-control.'[20] The Spirit of God enters into the church and into the hearts of individual Christians, transforming and restoring the human spirit corrupted by the Fall. It is through the Spirit that Christians find comfort as their suffering under the old order of the flesh gives way to the new spiritual existence of humanity reconciled with God. Through the work of the Spirit God brings to fulfilment the Christian hope that 'the whole creation itself might be freed from the slavery of corruption and brought into the same glorious freedom as the children of God.'[21]

Even such a brief and fragmentary account of the Christian narrative of salvation clearly distinguishes Christian spirituality from that embodied in the romantic / post-modern tradition. Theological liberalism begins and ends with the human spirit. It can accommodate the Christian narrative within its framework only by radically reconstructing it. For romanticism the Christian account of reality has its source not in divine revelation, but in human imagination and sensibility. Christian doctrine rejects this framework of interpretation: the human spirit can know God only through the authority of the Holy Spirit.

---

[19] Isaiah 11:1f.

[20] Galatians 5:22f.

[21] Romans 8:21.

The Christian Spiritual Life

Christian spirituality thus distinguishes the primacy of God's Spirit from the dependent reality of the human spirit. Within Christian theology, talk of human spirituality does not refer to an innate natural capacity for spiritual experience, since any such capacity has been eclipsed – to whatever degree – by the Fall. Rather, it refers to the developing relationship of the individual, within the Christian community, with God. The source and proper object of this relationship is not human introspection but grace known through divine revelation. Religious experience is thus contextualised within the Christian tradition upon which it is dependent. Thus Aumann defines theological reflection on Christian spirituality as

> that part of theology that, proceeding from the truths of divine revelation and the religious experience of individual persons, defines the nature of the supernatural life, formulates directives for its growth and development, and explains the process by which souls advance from the beginning of the spiritual life to its full perfection.[22]

The academic investigation of this particular facet of Christian teaching emerged as a separate and distinctive theological discipline only in the eighteenth century. Its terminology remains varied: 'spiritual theology', 'theology of Christian perfection', 'systematic theology of the spiritual life', 'ascetical theology' and 'mystical theology' are all used to refer to that aspect of the life of faith concerned with the Christian's 'spirituality', 'spiritual life', 'devout life', 'supernatural life', 'interior life' and 'mystical evolution'.

In the patristic age the term 'ascetic' was used to refer to the discipline of Christian living. The origins of asceticism are to be found in classical thought, in reference to any practical exercise or study devoted to the acquiring of a skill and achievement of virtue. The Christian life of prayer, worship and witness constituted a discipline that requires attention and training. With the emergence of monasticism such training became increasingly specialised, introducing a division between secular asceticism operating within society and religious asceticism functioning through a withdrawal from society. It was in the latter sphere that the notion of mystical theology emerged as a supplement and completion of ascetic theology. Beyond the public rites of the church stands a hidden reality,

---

[22] Aumann (1980), p.22.

beyond the literal meaning of scripture a deeper allegorical meaning, beyond positive theology a negative theology culminating in direct contemplation of the mystery of God.

Christian mysticism in the West was deeply influenced by the negative theology of Dionysius.[23] Monastic contemplative practices offered a path to the direct apprehension and communion with God that transcended the positive theology embodied in Christian doctrine. By understanding language and liturgy as a mediation of divine reality it was possible, through intensive programmes of spiritual discipline, to pass beyond mediatory artefacts and attain a mystical vision. However, Christian negative theology never bypasses positive theology, but rather works within it: negative theology is the fulfilment rather than the eclipse or negation of positive theology. If mystical experience is divorced from its positive theological roots then it leads into the very distortions of orthodox Christian spirituality represented by the romantic / post-modern tradition. This is of great significance, since advocates of the romantic / post-modern tradition frequently appeal to Christian, and other, mystical traditions in support of their universal claims.[24] Their case can only be made out if the tradition of negative theology is divorced from its necessary source in positive theological affirmation. Hence the tradition of negative theology can only be appealed to in a modernist context by reconstructing Christian orthodoxy.

Modern Catholic theology has sought both to preserve the continuity between ascetic theology and mystical theology, and hence the dependence of both on the objectivity of Christian revelation. 'There is but one path to Christian perfection, though it admits of ascetical and mystical stages, and the mystical life is not the result of extraordinary graces but the normal development and perfection of grace received by every Christian at baptism.'[25] Thus the Second Vatican Council affirms that Christian spirituality, whether or not it develops through a mystical negative stage, is necessarily grounded in the specific Christian revelation.

> The Lord Jesus, divine teacher and model of all perfection, preached holiness of life ... to each and every one of his disciples without distinction ... it is therefore quite clear that all Christians in any state or

---

[23] Dionysius Areopagita (1980).

[24] e.g. King (1995).

[25] Aumann (1980), p.15.

> walk of life are called to the fullness of Christian life and to the perfection of love ... the forms and tasks of life are many but holiness is one – that sanctity which is cultivated by all who act under God's Spirit and, obeying the Father's voice and adoring God the Father in spirit and truth, follow Christ, poor, humble and cross-bearing, that they may deserve to be partakers of his glory.[26]

Christian spirituality – as the liturgical, devotional, practical, social and political living out of the Christian life through the Holy Spirit, within the church as the body of Christ, in response to the revelation of the Trinitarian God – takes on many forms. It is here, indeed, that we encounter the cultural relativity of various forms of Christianity. Christian spirituality is informed by the diversity of Christian denominations: it is possible to speak of Catholic, Orthodox and Protestant spirituality, of Lutheran, Reformed, Evangelical and Pentecostal responses to the same revelation. It is also informed by geographical and historical location within time and space, hence the reality of African, Asian and Western forms of Christian spirituality, and of patristic, medieval and modern stages of its growth. Christian spiritual traditions may spring from more specific contexts: the leadership of individuals as in the Benedictine and Franciscan traditions; particular doctrinal concerns, as in biblical or sacramental styles of worship; or particular secular agendas, as in Christian feminism and forms of liberation theology.[27]

Despite their diversity, the varieties of Christian manifestations of the spiritual life have in common a response to Christian revelation that sets them apart from the romantic / post-modern tradition. Indeed, this tradition explicitly attempts to accommodate the various forms of Christian spirituality within its pseudo-universal framework by systematically dislocating them from their Trinitarian foundations. The fundamental issue at stake here is not whether the Christian tradition is either justifiable or true, merely the assertion that, if orthodox Christianity is understood within its historical and doctrinal integrity, it is revealed as being fundamentally incompatible with the spirituality currently taught to children in the majority of schools. It is, then, necessary to accept the reality of a diversity of contrasting and conflicting spiritual traditions.

---

[26] The Constitution on the Sacred Liturgy, n.2; quoted in Aumann (1980), p.15; cf. Flannery (1975).

[27] Wakefield (1983).

The claim is thus disproved that romantic / post-modern spiritual formulations are in continuity with the Christian tradition. The universalistic claims of such formulations are incompatible with Trinitarian orthodoxy, and this is revealed by the fact that to make such claims requires a reformulation of Christianity within a liberal experiential–expressive framework. This attempt at accommodation effectively shifts the foundations of Christian knowledge of God from divine revelation to human spiritual experience, which in turn ignores the reality that the source of Christian spirituality is the Holy Spirit, not the human spirit. Further, it relativises the fact that the spiritual life of the Christian is inevitably bound up with a commitment to a specific cultural and linguistic tradition that asserts realistic and exclusive truth claims. Only by reconstructing the Christian tradition may the romantic / post-modern tradition continue to affirm its universal status.

Part Three

Reconstruction:
Towards Spiritual Literacy

6. The Reality of Spiritual Diversity

In Part One an outline of the basic contours of the spiritual dimension within contemporary education was presented. The claim that this constitutes a universally valid understanding of spirituality was subject to a critique in Part Two: its origins in post-Enlightenment Western culture, together with its incompatibility with at least one other spiritual tradition – that of Trinitarian Christianity – suggest that this understanding of spirituality is a particular and localised one. In Part Three the focus shifts from that of description and critique to constructive reflection on the practical implications.

Trinitarian versus Romantic / Post-modern Spirituality

The preceding discussion has isolated two distinct forms of spirituality. First, there is a romantic / post-modern spirituality whose focus is on the inner experience of the individual. It is fundamentally suspicious of the tendency of modernity to impose inappropriate and hence pathological constraints on the spiritual life. Seeking freedom from such limitations, it attempts either the recovery of a lost dimension of transcendent experience, or the emancipation of the individual from any limiting meta-narrative. It holds that, by thus escaping from the constraints of modernity, an authentic inner spiritual life may be cultivated.

Secondly, there is a Christian spirituality grounded in the objective reality of the Trinitarian God. It is suspicious of the limitations of romantic and post-modern spirituality, finding in them a descent into a form of subjectivity that isolates the individual from any proper relationship with reality and is naively optimistic about the ability of individuals to achieve their own salvation. Spirituality here is not concerned with any transcendence of the natural order, but with the redemption of fallen creation: God, in the incarnation, reveals himself *within* the world of space and time. For the Christian, spirituality is concerned not with emancipation from the limitations imposed by nature and society, but with their transformation. The Christian life is one of pilgrimage into an authentic relationship with creation and the creator God. To be a Christian 'is to be incorporated into a community constituted by the stories of God', to have one's life interpreted by 'the narrative into which Christians are inscribed'.[1]

These two traditions reflect contrasting notions of human freedom. Romantic / post-modern freedom is concerned ultimately with emancipation from the constraints of the phenomenal world and the liberty to construct one's own inner reality. The Christian understanding of freedom is focused on the rejection of that false relationship with reality that results from sin, and the liberty to accept responsibility for authentic relationship – with the created order, with others in community, and ultimately with the Trinitarian God himself – in the light of the truths of divine revelation. A negative freedom-from-constraint is thus to be contrasted with a positive freedom-for-relationship within the order of creation.

As a result, each tradition offers contrasting interpretations of the nature and causes of the present spiritual crisis. From the perspective of romanticism and post-modernity the dogmatic assertion of the Trinitarian world view as exclusive realistic truth represents an authoritarian constraint on human freedom, one that functions both to create and perpetuate our spiritual malaise. For the orthodox Christian the flight of romanticism and post-modernity from the world, embodied in the belief that the only authentic relationship is constituted by inner self-reflection, creates a spiritual vacuum in which unconstrained freedom becomes pathological.

Attempts to accommodate either of these spiritual traditions within the structures of the other inevitably leads to a reductionism that operates in favour of the recipient. Thus to accommodate Christian spirituality within a romantic / post-modern framework ultimately undermines its essential Trinitarian structures. Trinitarian language – now understood not as a realistic depiction of objective reality but as a subjective expression of Christian religious experience – is made to function instrumentally as a way of establishing an immediate relationship with a sub-Christian Unitarian God. Here access to God is no longer mediated by Christ and the Holy Spirit: these are bypassed in favour of a direct experiential relationship between the individual and God. This process implies a

---

[1] Hauerwas (1995), p.137.

Unitarian theology that undermines the Trinitarian structures of Christianity by effectively rejecting the doctrines of the divinity of both the Son and the Holy Spirit. As a result the fundamental Christian distinction between the Spirit of God and the human spirit is blurred, allowing human spirituality to adopt the fiction of its own divinity. Consequently ultimate truth is discovered within the natural goodness of the individual and human spirituality becomes a form of self-contemplation rather than a developing relationship with the Creator.

Similarly the accommodation of romantic / post-modern spirituality within a Trinitarian framework entails a rejection of the process of emancipation from all ultimate truth claims in favour of the exclusive veracity of the Christian tradition. This leads in turn to the rejection of freedom understood as emancipation from all authority other than that of the autonomous self. Human spirituality becomes not an end in itself, but preparation for the reception of the truths of Christianity. Christianity accommodates romantic / post-modern spirituality within its own framework by understanding it as a move within natural theology, reflecting the universal human quest for God. 'The desire for God is written in the human heart ... men have given expression to their *quest for God* in their religious beliefs and behaviour: in their prayers, sacrifices, rituals, meditations and so forth.'[2] However, this quest cannot be completed by human effort; it does not achieve fulfilment until fallen creation is taken up, redeemed and sanctified by the God who reveals Himself as Father, Son and Holy Spirit: 'Only in God will he find the truth and happiness he never stops looking for.'[3]

Such a process of accommodation and synthesis thus ultimately fails. Christians are no more willing to give up their faith in the Trinitarian God than romantic / post-modernists are willing to accept that human spirituality achieves its ultimate goal in the actuality of the triune God. Unless one takes the distinctly anti-liberal and authoritarian step of enforcing such an accommodation, whether in favour of Christianity or post-modernism, there is no option but to affirm the reality of two incompatible spiritual traditions.

Given the near universal advocacy of the romantic / post-modern tradition in contemporary education it is difficult to avoid the conclusion, not

---

2 Catechism (1994), p.14, my italics.

3 ibid.

merely that the Christian tradition of spirituality has been eclipsed and disenfranchised, but that this has been achieved through a benign – though nevertheless highly capable – paternalistic authoritarianism. Children are taught to function effectively within the paradigm of the romantic / post-modern tradition, rather than to develop spiritual wisdom and insight in the light of a plurality of spiritual traditions. There is deep irony in this situation: children are nurtured into a single closed view of spirituality, in the name of their freedom and autonomy, by a tradition that prides itself in its open liberal credentials.

The Plurality of Spiritual Traditions in Contemporary Culture

The inevitable conclusion to be drawn from the preceding discussion is that education must come to terms with a plurality of spiritual traditions. The strategy of adopting HMI's anthropological definition as a universal formulation capable of locating spiritual plurality within a common framework must be deemed to have failed. This cannot be remedied merely by reintroducing HMI's theological definition alongside the anthropological one. Each of the major world faiths embodies a specific world view, a particular understanding of the nature of reality. As such they reflect distinctive spiritual traditions: it is necessary to speak of Christian, Hindu, Islamic, Jewish, Muslim and Sikh spirituality. These must be understood, in terms of their own inner integrity, as nominalistic. As such they are incapable of being accommodated within a generic framework, whether anthropological or theological, without distortion. Islam, for example, understands its spiritual tradition in the light of the revelation of the Qur'an, not merely as a particular, culturally relative, expression of a universal religious experience.

There is not the space here to unpack this plurality of spiritual traditions in any depth. The present argument is dependent only on the recognition of spiritual diversity. Nevertheless a brief account of the various spiritual traditions currently functioning in British society will help clarify the argument.[4]

---

[4] The typology that follows offers no more than a thumb-nail sketch; the rough percentages are taken from *Religions in the UK* (1993), pp.39ff.; cf. Bruce (1995); Francis & Kay (1995); Kay & Francis (1996); Shanks (1995); Thomas (1988).

Atheistic spirituality

About 30% of the population of Great Britain either do not believe in God or are agnostic about the existence of a transcendent realm. It is possible to identify here a range of secular spiritual traditions through which the human spirit seeks meaning and purpose within the confines of a closed universe. These range from humanistic affirmations of the worth, dignity and altruistic potential of the human species, through a variety of forms of stoic resignation, to a hedonistic search for pleasure and security limited by the immediate gratification offered by a consumer culture.

Religious spirituality

The remaining 70% of the population entertain some form of religious belief and identify themselves with a specific religious community: about 63% with a diversity of Trinitarian churches, and about 7% either with a world faith, new religious movement or non-Trinitarian church. Thus the great majority of the population work within spiritual traditions that find meaning and purpose through reference to a dimension of reality transcending the immanent framework of time and space. However only about 20% of the population admit to active membership of their religious communities, the rest retaining a nominal allegiance that is reflected in a loose – often heterodox and agnostic – adherence to the authoritative doctrines and practices of the various host communities. Hence it is appropriate to subdivide religious spirituality into that of the theologically committed and that of the religiously agnostic.

Theological spirituality

About 20% of the population choose an active and committed relationship with their host religious communities. Of these the most prevalent spiritual traditions are those of:

- Trinitarian Christians, in a diversity of denominational forms;
- other world faiths, especially those of Hindus, Muslims, Sikhs, Jews, Buddhists, Jains, Baha'is and Zoroastrians;
- adherents of non-Trinitarian churches and new religious movements.

Agnostic spirituality

The broad central band of about 50% of the population accept belief in some form of transcendence, often – at least when questioned – linking this with prevalent religious experience, but displaying no great enthusiasm for religious practice or any urgent need to differentiate between belief systems. Sociologically they reflect a variety of common, folk and civic religious attitudes. It is evident why the contemporary romantic / post-modern consensus, grounded in HMI's anthropological definition, should resonate with this particular cluster of spiritual traditions.

The Nature of Spirituality Revisited

The assertion that we must recognise a diversity of contrasting spiritual traditions, and so resist the temptation to assimilate them all within a romantic / post-modern framework, still recognises that they have enough in common for the designation 'spiritual' to be applied to all without undermining the integrity of any individual tradition. That is to say, the redefinition of spirituality developed in this section is *generic* in so far as it recognises a common aspect of our human existence in the world, but *nominalist* in so far as it allows each distinctive spiritual tradition to retain its individual integrity. On the basis of the perception that the point of contact between Trinitarian and romantic / post-modern spirituality is a common concern for that which is ultimate in the human condition, and in anticipation of the conclusions drawn later in the present section, the following definition of spirituality is now proposed.

> **Spirituality is the developing relationship of the individual, within community and tradition, to that which is – or is perceived to be – of ultimate concern, ultimate value and ultimate truth.**

Spirituality as development

Both romantic / post-modern and Trinitarian notions of spirituality accept its dynamic nature. Whether the rhetoric be that of a pilgrimage of faith or emancipation from cultural constraint, the spiritual life is essentially a process of movement towards an anticipated future. There is a tension between human experience as it is, and as it might be, that is at the heart of most, if not all, spiritual traditions. Spirituality thus has an eschatological dimension, informed by a sense of hope for future salvation or for greater depth of authentic existence. This does not, however, equate spiritual development with an evolutionary myth of necessary progress. Spiritual development can be retarded and pathological in nature.

Spirituality as relationship

Trinitarian spirituality seeks the establishment of proper relationships between the individual and society, the natural order and the divine realm. Similarly, the romantic / post-modern tradition is fundamentally concerned for the relationship of the individual with nature and culture. The fact that the understanding of what constitutes authentic relationship has still to be resolved is not of significance in the present context. Whether we choose speak of relationship in terms of *freedom-for*, or *freedom-from*, a key issue remains that of our relationship with ourselves, with others, with the world we indwell, and with the absence or presence of divinity.

Spirituality as individual and communal

Christian theology, drawing in the Trinitarian insight into God as a divine unity constituted by three persons in reciprocal relationship, understands personhood as being formed and constituted through mutual relationship with others. The individual's existence is always rooted within community. In contrast, the one aspect of modernity that romanticism and post-modernity have elected not to challenge has been its stress on the dislocated, isolated and autonomous individual, whose being is grounded not in mutual relationship but in self-reflection. Contemporary philosophy has embarked on a wholesale deconstruction of the viability of this picture. The individual committed to an autonomous existence freed from constraint inevitably retains a relationship with others in the romantic and post-modern cultural communities. If communal spirituality risks descending into a pathological following of the herd, so also autonomous spirituality is in danger of slipping into a solipsistic sickness. Spirituality thus involves a dynamic relationship between the individual and the community, and any affirmation of one aspect at the expense of the other would appear to be a retrograde move.

Spirituality and tradition

We understand the world through shared linguistic traditions. The notion that language is merely the expression of pre-linguistic experience, abstracted from received tradition, ignores the communal nature of language and the inevitability of our understanding operating within a distinct cultural context. Indeed, the notion of experience dislocated from tradition has itself come to form a specific tradition within modern thought. There is a dynamic relationship between experience and language. It is the shared language of stories, myths and narratives that shapes and forms our experience, while at the same time our broadening experience requires us to expand and refine our linguistic heritage. The pupil in the classroom indwells a linguistic tradition, and is in possession of an understanding of ultimate value and truth, however ill-defined and incoherent this may be.

Spiritual perception

The distinction between 'that which is' and 'that which is perceived to be' in our definition of spirituality is crucial. It raises the possibility that spiritual perception of reality may be either false or true; that spirituality may be either authentic or inauthentic. Merely extending the pupils' depth and quality of experiential spiritual perception does not guarantee a mature spirituality. The racist spirituality of extreme political groupings, together with the spirituality of a rampant capitalist money culture, thrive equally by cultivating a depth of sensitivity and desire that is open to manipulation and abuse. The issue of the relationship between reality-as-it-is-in-itself and reality-as-it-is-perceived forms an area of contention between Christian and post-modern spirituality. For the post-modernist there is no reality in itself, only reality as is appears to us, or as we choose to construct it. For the Christian the only true reality is that of God and his creation, and these exist regardless of whether or not human beings actually perceive them. We are thus faced with a polarity between realistic and exclusive truth on the one hand, and relative and anti-realistic truth on the other. This however does not make the issue of truth itself optional. Post-modernity, in so far as it rejects all meta-narratives, actually produces its own: the meta-narrative that proclaims the truth that there is no truth. Neither is the decision about truth necessarily one of a choice between absolute certainty and absolute ambiguity. Christianity, for example, recognises that positive theology requires negative theology, that affirmative theological statements always fall short of the divine reality. Consequently it follows the path of contingent rationality, of faith seeking understanding. The present definition of spirituality does not require a resolution of these issues, merely the recognition that any spiritual tradition must inevitably, whether implicitly or explicitly, work with an understanding of the actual order of reality and of the nature of our knowledge concerning it.

Spirituality and ultimate concern

For most of our lives our concerns are parochial ones: the need to study hard to pass an exam, the need to find ways of better motivating a class, the need to publish good examination results at the end of the academic year. Implicit behind these is a series of more fundamental ultimate concerns: what do I want out of life; what is the ultimate meaning and purpose of my existence? A healthy spiritual life is one in which ultimate concerns are reflected on frequently and in depth, and which has a profound influence on the way parochial concerns are dealt with. The pupil whose motivation to pass an exam is a deeper one than merely pleasing her or his parents or guardians, the teacher whose vocation demands the best standards of teaching, the school community whose educational values transcend those of mere competition: these all point towards a vision of spiritual integrity. The 1988 Education Reform Act requires that schools take responsibility for the spiritual development of pupils and of society. They must provide for the educational development of the ultimate concerns, not merely of the school as a community, but of the broader society. It becomes clear why there is such a close connection between Religious Education and spirituality: it is difficult to ask a more ultimate question than that of the existence, or non-existence, of God.[5]

Spirituality and ultimate value

Our values flow from our concerns. The extent to and manner in which we value ourselves, those around us, our environment and the absence or presence of God is dependent on the level of concern we have about them. It is not a matter of establishing morality, and thereby creating the context in which we are free to indulge in the luxury of asking ultimate questions. Consequently spiritual education can never be appropriated merely as an instrument of moral progress. The task of promoting moral development allotted to schools by the Education Reform Act demands a material content, a vision of exactly what moral development and the common good entails. This question cannot be answered unless society is clear about its ultimate concerns. Spirituality thus takes priority over morality. If this argument is correct then the moral maze in which society finds itself, and for which education is often made the scapegoat, may be seen as a direct result of a deeper spiritual malaise.

---

[5] Tillich comes close to equating these two: the question of God and the question of our ultimate concern are one and the same; cf. Wright (1993), pp.44f.

Spirituality and ultimate truth

At the heart of spirituality is the question of truth. Are our spiritual lives attuned to the way things actually are in the world, or are they in dissonance with reality? Such a statement is, of course, not a fashionable one to make in the context of an emerging post-modern culture. Yet at the heart of the spiritual malaise of society is the fact that questions of truth are, through a variety of strategies, effectively bypassed. Truth is privatised, ridiculed, relativised, patronised and ignored. Yet the essence of our spiritual lives, the core of our collective humanity, the motivation of scientist and artist, is precisely the desire for that truth from which all else flows.

The educational dilemma is how to teach spirituality in a cultural context in which spiritual truth matters, in which the power and influence of pathological spiritual traditions are recognised, yet in which there is no consensus as to which, if any, truth is ultimately real and authentic. The ambiguity of this situation does not negate the need for individuals and communities to make spiritual decisions about ultimate truth and value. Such judgements are an inevitable part of everyday existence, and in a pluralistic society will be various, reflecting the diversity of spiritual traditions that constitute the nation's cultural heritage. In this context, to limit the criteria for such judgements to either the prejudice of personal preference, or the accident of induction into a particular cultural tradition, seems an inadequate response. Rather, the educational task needs to be seen in terms of developing the literacy of individuals, and of society as a whole, so as to enable the collective spiritual pilgrimage towards proper relationship with that which is indeed ultimately true and of ultimate value to proceed with wisdom, insight and intelligence.

This chapter has set out – prior to a consideration of the educational implications – to map the contours of the plurality of spiritual traditions prevalent within contemporary society. Its comparison of the Trinitarian and romantic / post-modern traditions supported the suggestion that education must take spiritual diversity seriously. Three broad clusters of contemporary spirituality – atheistic, theological and agnostic – were then identified, and finally a working definition of spirituality was offered that claimed to be generic in form yet nominalist in material content.

7. The Task of Spiritual Education

The concern of this final chapter is to begin to explore the possibilities of implementing a programme of spiritual education against the background of:

- the recognition of a plurality of spiritual traditions;

- the revised definition of spirituality outlined in the previous chapter; and

- the legal structures of the 1988 Education Reform Act.

Models of Education

Modernity was driven by a hermeneutic of suspicion: only by stripping away received tradition, dislocating the self from external authority, and cultivating rational autonomy could the individual achieve emancipation from illusion. This isolationist process was reinforced by the modernist distinction between fact and value, embodied in the liberal affirmation of freedom of belief. Under the shadow of the hermeneutic of suspicion we are emancipated from the authority of tradition and hence free to believe whatever we like, the only limitations being that we do not attempt to impose our beliefs upon others through any authoritarian or violent means, and that we respect and tolerate the beliefs of others.

Romanticism and post-modernism take this agenda to its logical conclusion. Since individuals possess conflicting beliefs concerning the ultimate nature of reality, there can only ever be a plurality of incommensurable world views. Consequently the moral task becomes that of emancipating individuals from cultural constraint in order to maximise their freedom to create their own personal reality. This is precisely the programme adopted by the contemporary consensus surrounding spiritual education.

In the context of education it was through a progressive child-centred pedagogy, first articulated by Rousseau, that this hermeneutic of suspicion was applied. For Rousseau education consists 'not in teaching virtue or truth, but in preserving the heart from vice and from the spirit of error.'[1] Progressive education seeks to enable the child to achieve a natural moral development through a negative education that sets out to protect her or him from the corruption threatened by a polluted cultural heritage. In its post-modern form such a negative education aims to cultivate the habit of freedom by encouraging the pupil to transcend the meta-narratives of modernity and seize the freedom of desire through which the rich diversity of cultural symbols and artefacts may be embraced and celebrated without the threat of constraint.[2]

Effectively such an pedagogy leaves children in a moral and intellectual vacuum in which they are forced to fall back on their own resources. A moral dimension can be present within this vacuum only if the romantic belief that 'the first impulses of nature are always right; there is no original sin in the human heart'[3] is true. Clearly this is a matter of contention: it is by no means certain that, if space is created for the child to develop in such an idealised environment, the results will be a child imbued with natural goodness and spiritual insight. Further, it is naive to suggest that the creation of such a vacuum is possible. The reality is that such programmes of negative education actually function by nurturing and inducting children into romantic and post-modern world views. Here the romantic meta-narrative that provides the foundation of such educational programmes is not open to negotiation, but is simply taken for granted. Hence Gay's suggestion that educators found themselves 'led through the devious and embarrassing detours of repression and manipulation that were a denial and mockery of the world they hoped to bring into being.'[4]

At the other end of the educational spectrum from that of Rousseau's negative education stands the traditionalist model associated with John Locke. Here education is wholly positive and driven by a hermeneutic of trust. Moral development is achieved through the substance of the educational process itself. 'Of all men we meet with, nine parts of ten are

---

[1] Rousseau (1986), p.57.

[2] Usher and Edwards (1994).

[3] Rousseau, op. cit., p.56.

[4] Gay (1973b), p.497

what they are, good or evil, useful or not, by their education.'[5] The task of education is to induct children into the moral and intellectual heritage of society. It is this educational model that lies behind the 1988 Education Reform Act.

Here the personal formation of the individual is dependent on a developing relationship with society and culture. The child simply cannot avoid learning from the context of education: the values, attitudes and spiritual life of the school as a learning community will inevitably, and for good or ill, influence the pupil. It is not a question here of a choice between negative and positive education, since both progressive and traditionalist educational programmes effectively induct children into a particular world view. Rather the choice is between which particular value systems and spiritual traditions children are to be inducted into.

The implications of this argument will be drawn out in the next section. Here it is sufficient to underline the provisional conclusion.

Education will inevitably nurture children into a particular world view. The question is not whether this will happen, but how: consequently a primary task of spiritual education is to ensure that the spiritual tradition in which children are nurtured is appropriate, and that the process of nurture is effective.

Such a position will, undoubtedly, deeply concern many liberal educators who identify with progressive models. Is the proposal not merely a neo-conservative licence to impose on children a particular value system? Is education not reduced to a form of indoctrination and social engineering? Hirst has provided the most significant articulation of these concerns. Education that is merely induction into culture leaves children vulnerable to historical chance: the traditions into which they are inducted will be fundamentally determined by the cultural context into which they are born.

For Hirst the dilemma could be avoided by grounding education not on the process of a transmission of a relativistic culture but on the objectivity of knowledge itself. The problem here is that it is by no means clear that human knowledge can simply be withdrawn from its cultural context and attributed with an objective trans-cultural status. Will not attempts to do so

---

[5] Locke (1968), p.114.

simply impose an alternative relativistic cultural tradition that hides behind a rhetoric of universality?[6]

The debate between Hirst and traditionalist education tends towards a polarisation: either knowledge is absolute and universal, or it is culturally relative. An alternative possibility is to understand knowledge in terms of development and progress. Here knowledge has as much to do with the means by which human beings reach understanding as the concrete results they achieve. This entails the adoption of an understanding of the contingent nature of rationality. To be knowledgeable and informed about a subject is not to possess fixed results, but to be aware of, and able to take a part in the process of developing and refining human insight in that particular sphere. In other words, knowledge entails the ability to think intelligently and wisely about an object, and enter into communication with others about it. Knowledge here has to do fundamentally with degrees of literacy.

Spirituality, as we have seen, constitutes an ambiguous realm of human knowledge and understanding. There is a diversity of contrasting and competing traditions of spirituality. A critical spiritual education does not need to make a stark choice between the transmission of a relativistic culturally determined tradition and one that lays claim to universality. Either option will, inevitably, limit the pupils' understanding of the reality of the ambiguous status of our spiritual knowledge. Rather a critical spiritual education will give children access to the diversity of spiritual options available, together with the skills and insights through which they can enter into contemporary debate and learn how to differentiate and make informed judgements between a variety of possibilities. The achievement of such spiritual literacy thus moves beyond a paternalistic induction into a single tradition. Consequently it is not inevitable that the pupils' understanding of spirituality is simply transcribed by the limits of the spiritual tradition within which the school operates.

Alongside a hermeneutic of trust must stand a hermeneutic of suspicion.

---

[6] We have already seen how this process has occurred within spiritual education. The claim for universality made by the romantic / post-modern tradition is fundamentally flawed. Rather than avoiding the possibility of inducting children into a particular spiritual tradition the contemporary consensus achieves precisely that outcome.

In addition to nurturing pupils within a particular spiritual tradition the school also has the duty of allowing them critical access to alternative traditions so that informed insight and wisdom may flourish through the development of spiritual literacy.

This leaves unaddressed the question of the relationship between a hermeneutic of trust and one of suspicion. How are nurture and critical insight to function together within a single community? The proposal here is that a distinction is made between the Whole Curriculum and the Basic Curriculum, as these are laid down by the Education Reform Act. The end of spiritual education will be that of the spiritual development of the child in community. This will be achieved through two complementary processes. Firstly, within the Whole Curriculum – through the fundamental aims of the school, its spiritual ethos and the celebration of this through Collective Worship – children will be inducted and nurtured within a particular spiritual tradition. Secondly, within the Basic Curriculum – through the teaching of specific subject areas and cross-curricular themes – children will have the opportunity to develop a religious literacy in which the spiritual traditions of the school are opened up for critical investigation in the light of alternatives. The fundamental concern here will not be to utilise the learning process instrumentally as a means of confirming and reinforcing the process of spiritual nurture, but to develop children's ability to take informed responsibility for their own spiritual development.

Education as Spiritual Nurture

Any consideration of the task of spiritual nurture in schools must take account of the polarisation in educational provision that has developed since the 1988 Education Reform Act. On the one hand, responsibility for the fundamental aims and material content of education has passed to central government. Schools are free to choose neither what they teach, nor the reasons for doing so. On the other hand, this process of centralisation has not been accompanied by a reinforcement of comprehensive schooling. Schools are increasingly autonomous communities with independent responsibility for the local implementation of national legislation. Thus they have an individual responsibility to interpret the legal requirement that they attend to the spiritual development of their pupils according to their specific context.

Since there is no universal understanding of the nature of spirituality, and since clearly legislation in this area is not merely open to, but also requires, interpretation, it becomes the responsibility of the school to make decisions regarding the spiritual tradition that informs the Whole Curriculum. A school with spiritual integrity must take this responsibility seriously. This requires the development of a communal agreement between pupils, staff, management, governors, parents and the local community concerning the fundamental spiritual values to which the school is committed. The more explicit and secure its spiritual outlook, the more its fundamental values are explicitly acknowledged and celebrated within the community, the greater the spiritual authenticity.

These spiritual values will then need to be transmitted: through policy statements, through academic and pastoral practices, through the developing ethos of the school, and through Collective Worship. The danger here will be that more parochial concerns will cloud the genuine spiritual foundations of the community. This is classically true in the area of Collective Worship. It is here, above all, that the spiritual core of the school needs to be articulated, affirmed and celebrated. However, all too often such worship reflects a series of parochial compromises in which, often in an attempt to pay lip service to the law, a diversity of beliefs and outlooks are welded together into an uncomfortable middle-ground consensus that pleases few and leaves the heart of the school's life in a state of ambiguity. Thus pupils are nurtured in the view that spirituality is not something to be celebrated but something to be slightly embarrassed about. In terms of the legal options open to a school there seems to be very little excuse for perpetuating such ambiguity. It is quite possible, for example, for a school to opt out of the requirements of Collective Worship, and replace this with an assembly in which the spiritual life of the school can be celebrated without recourse to any predetermined framework.

It is perhaps in denominational schools, particularly Anglican ones, that the danger of pupils being nurtured in unsatisfactory modes of spirituality is most prevalent. The Anglican tradition of educational service to the broader community, as opposed to service to the children of Anglican parents, may be seen as a root cause of this dilemma. Since the ethos of an Anglican school is often directed towards service beyond the boundaries of the Christian community, the concern to avoid any hint of indoctrination has led many schools to adopt a broad moral agenda that effectively compromises the Trinitarian spiritual foundations upon which the school is established. Consequently children are often given the spiritual message that Christianity is a good thing but that this is not necessarily a cause for communal celebration. Indeed, it is difficult to distinguish any specifically Anglican spirituality underlying some Anglican discussions of spirituality in church schools. It may simply be that the Anglican tradition of service to the community is outdated and requires revision. Given the existence of state provision for the education of all children, the notion of service through providing church schools now appears redundant. It may be that the true service that Anglican schools may offer to the nation is the unambiguous celebration of a distinctive, though now minority, spiritual tradition.

Spirituality, we have suggested, has to do with our embodied relationship with that which is of ultimate truth and value. Further, we learn through our place within the community, and our spiritual understanding is influenced by those with whom we live and work and the cultural traditions we inherit. Schools will inevitably transmit their understanding of spirituality: an impression of what, for that particular community, is ultimately true and of fundamental value. Given the diversity of spiritual perspectives it is simply common sense that schools should be pro-active in recognising, articulating, developing and transmitting a set of spiritual values, and in nurturing children into a received spiritual tradition.

The school community will thus nurture its pupils into its values, aims and ultimate spiritual commitments. Since such a process is inevitable, it makes sense for a school to attend to this issue and to see it as something worthy of unapologetic celebration. The hermeneutic of suspicion has, all too often, caused schools to hesitate before affirming and transmitting their core values. The rhetoric of encouraging children to discover for themselves bypasses the legacy of spiritual wisdom and insight that is the child's rightful inheritance.

Education for Spiritual Wisdom

However, if spiritual education stops at this point then it will be found wanting. The reality that spiritual development is grounded in unapologetic nurture is not justification for making the process the sole source of spiritual education. The spiritual issues of ultimate truth and ultimate value are the subject of intense dispute and controversy within contemporary society, and consequently schools have a duty to enable children to respond with informed wisdom to such ambiguity. A spiritual education that begins and ends with mere nurture limits pupils' understanding and insight, and becomes simply a form of cultural transmission that verges on indoctrination. The hermeneutic of faith demands to be balanced with a hermeneutic of suspicion.

The failure of schools to attend to the critical dimension of spiritual education has been clearly outlined in the first part of this study. The policy development that shifted spirituality out of the curriculum itself into the basic statement of educational aims plays a significant role in this process. The search for consensus in the early development of spiritual education reflected a need not to investigate the plurality of spiritual traditions but to adopt a universal perspective into which children could be inducted. The suggestion made here is that spirituality as an object of critical study must recover its proper place within the curriculum. Alongside the process of nurture must stand a tradition of investigation, critique and examination.

Since current legislation understands the spiritual dimension as permeating all of the school's life, such critical investigation must form part of the curriculum of all subject areas. This is not to suggest that each subject area should be required to pay equal attention to this dimension of education. The case that all of Religious Education should address the spiritual dimension can relatively easily be made out. Phenomenologically, the essence of an item of religious culture, that which justifies labelling it as 'religious', is its attention to the sphere of transcendence. In asking the question of the nature of transcendent reality one inevitably raises ultimate spiritual issues of fact and value. Mathematics, on the other hand, is less likely to be concerned on a day-to-day basis with ultimate questions. That is not to deny that mathematics as a discipline may raise fundamental philosophical, and indeed theological questions, merely to affirm that such questions are not to be found at the cutting edge of the mathematics curriculum, at least not at primary and secondary levels. Between these extremes the other subject disciplines – English, history, geography, science, languages, etc. – all, inevitably, raise ultimate questions. An analysis of the motivation of a character in a short story, or of the history of British colonialism, or of the nature of scientific truth, all inevitably push the child into reflecting on ultimate spiritual issues.

The answers to such questions raised within the curriculum cannot be simply pre-packaged. The naiveté of public educational debate in the United States of America, with its ongoing battle between creationism and evolution, reflects a poverty of educational insight. Its concern is fundamentally with a power struggle over which 'truth' children should be taught. An educational programme with integrity will offer both sides of the argument and allow children to develop an informed and literate understanding of the issues, whatever their personal beliefs and convictions. Children need to be made aware of the diversity of spiritual traditions operating within society, they need to be offered the resources whereby they can identify and refine their developing relationship with the tradition in which they were brought up, and which they must, inevitably, elect either to accept or reject. They must also have access to an informed understanding of the plurality of alternative world-views and spiritual traditions, and they must feel the power of alternative truth claims and alternative value systems. The conflict that may result between a variety of alternatives is to be welcomed and celebrated. It has long been recognised that there is no growth without struggle, no move towards spiritual depth and integrity without a wrestling with ultimate questions.

Children come to lessons already indwelling a spiritual tradition, already in possession of a set of ultimate beliefs and values, however poorly articulated and inadequately formed these might be. This pre-understanding will be reinforced and developed by the process of spiritual nurture. Critical spiritual education entails the process of bringing such pre-understanding into constructive dialogue with alternative spiritual traditions, in a manner in which children can appreciate the spiritual beliefs and values of others in the process of refining and developing their own. This will require the development of spiritual literacy, of the skills needed for pupils to take their place in society informed, articulate, sensitive and engaged with spiritual issues.

There can be little doubt that the promise of modern culture has not been realised. Its distinction between the realms of fact and value produced a world bereft of spiritual insight. Children were cast adrift from the wisdom of tradition; left isolated and dislocated in a materialistic world. The romantic tradition fought bravely to remedy this situation, seeking to recover a lost dimension of spiritual value. However, it failed to root spiritual experience in any cultural or communal context. As a result it quickly collapsed into a post-modern culture in which children are free to create the reality they choose, on the basis of personal desire, inclination and preference. Ultimately this leaves children prey to manipulation by cultural forces they are ill equipped either to recognise or to counter. The spiritual sterility of the romantic / post-modern tradition mirrors that of modernism. Any authentic spirituality requires the twin foundations of roots and discernment. The roots are made available through a hermeneutic of faith in which society does not withhold, in the misplaced name of the child's 'freedom', a spirituality that has passed through the historical crucible of testing and refinement. Discernment is made available through a hermeneutic of suspicion in which children are provided with the skills to recognise, understand and judge within the spiritual plurality that forms the current legacy of the Western world.

Genuine spiritual education thus transcends the limitations of a pedagogy concerned with stimulating the child's experiential sensitivity as an end in itself. It demands the embodiment of questions of ultimate truth within developing traditions, an awareness of the spiritual ambiguity of a society that functions with a diversity of spiritual traditions, and the ability to develop one's own spiritual life with wisdom and insight.

Bibliography

Government Documents

HMSO (1944) *Education Reform Act*, London: HMSO.

DES (1977) *Education in Our Schools*, London: HMSO.

DES / HMI (1977a) *Curriculum 11–16*, London: HMSO.

DES / HMI (1977b) *Supplement to Curriculum 11–16*, London: HMSO.

DES (1979) *LEA Arrangements for the School Curriculum*, London: DES.

DES / HMI (1980) *A View of the Curriculum*, London: HMSO.

APU (1981) *Personal and Social Development*, London: DES.

DES (1981) *The School Curriculum*, London: HMSO.

DES (1985a) *The Curriculum from 5 to 16. Curriculum Matters 2*, London: DES.

DES (1985b) *Better Schools*, London: DES.

HMSO (1985) *Education for All: The Report of the Committee of Inquiry into the Education of Children from Ethnic Minority Groups* (The Swann Report), London: HMSO.

HMSO (1986) *Education (No. 2) Act*, London: HMSO.

DES (1987) *The National Curriculum 5–16*, London: HMSO.

HMSO (1988) *Education Reform Act*, London: HMSO.

DFE (1992) *Choice and Diversity*, London: HMSO.

HMSO (1993) *Education Act*, London: HMSO.

NCC (1993) *Spiritual and Moral Development,* York: NCC.

OFSTED (1993) *The Handbook for the Inspection of Schools,* London: DFE.

DFE (1994) *Religious Education and Collective Worship.* Circular 1/94, London: DFE.

OFSTED (1994a) *Spiritual, Moral, Social and Cultural Development,* London: DFE.

OFSTED (1994b) *Religious Education and Collective Worship 1992–93,* London: DFE.

SCAA (1994a) *The National Curriculum and its Assessment,* London: SCAA.

SCAA (1994b) *Model Syllabuses for Religious Education,* London: SCAA.

SCAA (1995a) *Religious Education 16–19,* London: SCAA.

SCAA (1995b) *Spiritual and Moral Development. SCAA Discussion Papers: No. 3,* London: SCAA.

General Bibliography

Adorno, T.W. and Horkheimer, M. (1972) *Dialectic of Enlightenment.* New York: Herder & Herder.

Agger, B. (1991) *A Critical Theory of Public Life: Knowledge, Discourse and Politics in an Age of Decline.* London: Falmer Press.

Agger, B. (1992) *Cultural Studies as Critical Theory.* London: Falmer Press.

Alcock, J. (1993) 'Spirituality, Religious Education and the Dramatic Arts: Occasions of Comfort and Celebration' in Starkings, D. (ed.) *Religion and the Arts in Education: Dimensions of Spirituality.* London: Hodder & Stoughton, pp.169–178.

Alves, C. (1991) 'Just a Matter of Words? The Religious Education Debate in the House of Lords'. *British Journal of Religious Education,* 13:3, pp.168–174.

Archambault, R.D. (ed.) (1965) *Philosophical Analysis and Education.* London: Routledge & Kegan Paul.

Ashraf, S.A. (1992) 'The Religious Approach to Religious Education: The Methodology of Awakening and Disciplining the Religious Sensibility' in Watson, B. (ed.) *Priorities in Religious Education. A Model for the 1990s and Beyond.* London: Falmer Press, pp.81–91.

Association of Christian Teachers. (1989) *Spiritual Development – How Is It To Be Understood And Promoted?* ACT Briefing Paper No 1, London: ACT

Astley, J. and Francis, L.J. (eds) (1996) *Christian Theology and Religious Education: Connections and Contradictions.* London: SPCK.

Attfield, D.G. (1996) 'Learning from Religion'. *British Journal of Religious Education*, 18:2, pp.78–84.

Attridge, S. (1993) 'Fictions of Other Cultures' in Starkings, D. (ed.) *Religion and the Arts in Education: Dimensions of Spirituality.* London: Hodder & Stoughton, pp.45–54.

Aumann, J. (1980) *Spiritual Theology.* London: Sheed & Ward.

Avis, P. (1986) *The Methods of Modern Theology: The Dream of Reason.* Basingstoke: Marshall Pickering.

Baldwin, G. (1996) 'Modern Spirituality, Moral Education and the History Curriculum' in Best, R. (ed.) *Education, Spirituality and the Whole Child.* London: Cassell, pp.206–221.

Bantock, G.H. (1980) *Studies in the History of Educational Theory. Volume One. Artifice and Nature 1350–1765.* London: Allen and Unwin.

Barbour, I.G. (ed.) (1968) *Science and Religion: New Perspectives on the Dialogue.* London: SCM.

Barrow, R. and White, P. (eds) (1993) *Beyond Liberal Education. Essays in Honour of Paul H. Hirst.* London: Routledge.

Barth, K. (1980) *The Epistle to the Romans.* Oxford: Oxford University Press.

Barth, K. and Brunner, E. (1946) *Natural Theology.* London: SCM.

Bartley, W.W. (1964) *The Retreat to Commitment.* Illinois: Open Court.

Bates, D. (1982) 'Lancaster Religious Education: An Appraisal' in Webster, D.H., and Tickner, M.F. (eds) *Religious Education and the Imagination. Aspects of Education: 28.* Hull: University of Hull Institute of Education, pp.22–36.

Bauman, Z. (1994) *Postmodern Ethics.* Oxford: Blackwell.

Bausor, J., Black, P., Poole, M., and Woolnough, B. (1995) 'Keep Your Spirits Up', *Times Education Supplement.* December 29, p. xi.

Beesley, M. (1993) 'Spiritual Education in Schools'. *Pastoral Care*, 11:3, pp.22–27.

Berger, P. and Luckmann, T. (1967*) The Social Construction of Reality*. Harmondsworth: Penguin Books.

Bernstein, R.J. (1983) *Beyond Objectivism and Relativism: Science, Hermeneutics and Praxis.* Oxford: Basil Blackwell.

Berry, P. and Wernick, A. (eds) (1992) *Shadow of Spirit: Postmodernism and Religion.* London: Routledge.

Berryman, J.W. (1985) 'Children's Spirituality and Religious Language'. *British Journal of Religious Education.* 7:3, pp.120–127.

Best, R. (ed.) (1996) *Education, Spirituality and the Whole Child.* London: Cassell.

Bowen, J. (1981) *A History of Western Education. Volume Three. The Modern West.* London: Methuen.

Boyne, R. (1990*) Foucault and Derrida. The Other Side of Reason.* London: Unwin Hyman.

Bradford, J. (1995) *Caring for the Whole Child: A Holistic Approach to Spirituality.* London: The Children's Society.

Brown, A. (1995) 'Changing the agenda: whose agenda?'. *British Journal of Religious Education,* 17:3, pp.148–156.

Brown, A. and Furlong, J. (1996) *Spiritual Development in Schools. Invisible to the Eye.* London: National Society.

Bruce, S. (1995) *Religion in Modern Britain.* Oxford: OUP.

Buckley, M. (1987) *The Roots of Modern Atheism.* New Haven: Yale University Press.

Burn, J. and Hart, C. (1988) *The Crisis in Religious Education.* London: Educational Research Trust.

Callaghan, J. (1976) 'Towards a National Debate'. *Education,* 148:17, pp.132–133.

Calvin, J. (1960) *Institutes of the Christian Religion. Volume One.* Philadelphia: Westminster Press.

Cassirer, E. (1951) *The Philosophy of the Enlightenment.* Princeton: Princeton University Press.

Catechism of the Catholic Church (1994) London: Geoffrey Chapman.

Chambers, F.P. (1932) *A History of Taste.* New York: Columbia University Press.

Clark, H. (1993) *The Church Under Thatcher.* London: SPCK.

Clark, V. (1995) 'Childhood Bereavement and Spiritual Growth: First Steps in Exploring Some Issues'. *SPES,* 3, pp.2–10.

Clarke, S. (1995) 'Spirituality in Education: a Buddhist Perspective'. *SPES,* 3, pp.15–18.

Clements, R.E. (1978) *Old Testament Theology. A Fresh Approach.* London: Marshall, Morgan and Scott.

Coward, H. and Foshay, T. (eds) (1992) *Derrida and Negative Theology.* Albany: State University of New York Press.

Cox, E. (1983) 'Understanding Religion and Religious Understanding'. *British Journal of Religious Education,* 6:1, pp.3–7, 13.

Cox, E. and Cairns, J. (1989) *Reforming Religious Education: the religious clauses of the 1988 Education Reform Act.* London: Kogan Page.

Crawford, M. and Rossiter, G. (1996) 'School education and the spiritual development of adolescents: an Australian perspective' in Best, R. (ed.) *Education, Spirituality and the Whole Child.* London: Cassell, pp.305–318.

Cupitt, D. (1987) *The Long-legged Fly. A Theology of Language and Desire.* London: SCM.

Cupitt, D. (1991) *What is a Story?* London: SCM.

D' Costa, G. (ed.) (1990) *Christian Uniqueness Reconsidered. The Myth of a Pluralistic Theology of Religions.* New York: Orbis Books.

Dahlhaus, C. (1993) *Ludwig van Beethoven: Approaches to His Music.* Oxford: Clarendon.

Darling, J. (1986) 'Child-centred, Gender-centred: a criticism of progressive education from Rousseau to Plowden'. *Oxford Review of Education,* 12:1, p.31–40.

Day, D. (1985) 'Religious Education Forty Years On: A Permanent Identity Crisis?' *British Journal of Religious Education,* 7:2, pp.55–63.

Derrida, J. (1976) *Of Grammatology.* Baltimore: Johns Hopkins University Press.

Derrida, J. (1978) *Writing and Difference.* Chicago: Chicago University Press.

Derrida, J. (1982) *Margins of Philosophy.* London: Harvester Wheatsheaf.

Desai, A. (1995) 'Spirituality: Humanist and Metaphysical Perspectives'. *Resource,* 17:2, pp.12–13.

Descartes, R. (1970) *Philosophical Writings.* London: Nelson University Paperbacks.

Dionysius Areopagita [Pseudo-Dionysius] (1980) *The Divine Names and The Mystical Theology.* Milwaukee: Marquette University Press.

Dunn, J.D.G. (1975) *Jesus and the Spirit. A Study of the Religious and Charismatic Experiences of Jesus and the First Christians as Reflected in the New Testament.* London: SCM.

Durka, G. and Smith, J. (eds) (1979) *Aesthetic Dimensions of Religious Education.* London: Paulist Press.

Eliot, T.S. (1974) *Collected Poems 1909–1962.* London: Faber & Faber.

Erricker, C. (1993) 'The Iconic Quality of the Mind' in Starkings, D. (ed.) *Religion and the Arts in Education: Dimensions of Spirituality.* London: Hodder & Stoughton, pp.138–147.

Erricker, C. and Erricker, J. (1996) 'Where Angels Fear to Tread: Discovering Children's Spirituality' in Best, R. (ed.) *Education, Spirituality and the Whole Child.* London: Cassell, pp.184–195.

Evers, C.W. (1987) 'Epistemology and the Structure of Educational Theory: some reflections on the O'Connor–Hirst debate'. *Journal of Philosophy of Education,* 21:1, pp.3–13.

Fackenheim, E.L. (1985) 'Immanuel Kant' in Smart, N., Clayton, N., et al. (eds) *Nineteenth-century Religious Thought in the West. Volume One.* Cambridge: Cambridge University Press, pp.17–40.

Felderhof, M. (ed.) (1984) *RE in a Pluralistic Society.* Sevenoaks: Hodder & Stoughton Educational.

Feuerbach, L. (1989) *The Essence of Christianity.* New York: Prometheus Books.

Flannery, A. (1975) *Vatican Council II: The Conciliar and Post-Conciliar Documents.* Northport, New York: Costello Publishing.

Flude, M. and Hammer, M. (eds) (1990) *The Education Reform Act 1988. Its Origins and Implications.* London: Falmer Press.

Foucault, M. (1989) *The Order of Things. An Archaeology of the Human Sciences.* London: Tavistock / Routledge.

Foucault, M. (1991) *The Archaeology of Knowledge.* London: Routledge.

Francis, L. and Thatcher, A. (eds) (1990) *Christian Perspectives for Education.* Leominster: Gracewing / Fowler Wright.

Francis, L.J. and Kay, W.K. (1995) *Teenage Religion and Values*. Leominster: Gracewing.

Francis, L.J. and Lankshear, D.W. (eds) (1993) *Christian Perspectives on Church Schools: A Reader*. Leominster: Gracewing / Fowler Wright.

Francis, L.J., Kay, W.K. and Campbell, W.S. (eds) (1996) *Research In Religious Education*. Leominster: Gracewing / Fowler Wright.

Gadamer , H.-G. (1979) *Truth and Method*. London: Sheed and Ward.

Gasche, R. (1986) *The Tain of the Mirror. Derrida and the Philosophy of Reflection*. C. Massachusetts: Harvard University Press.

Gay. P. (1973a) *The Enlightenment. An Interpretation. One: The Rise of Modern Paganism*. London: Wildwood House.

Gay. P. (1973b) *The Enlightenment. An Interpretation. Two: The Science of Freedom*. London: Wildwood House.

Gearon, L. (1995) 'What is Metaphysics? Postmodern Hermeneutics and Religious Education'. *Journal of Beliefs and Values*, 16:1, pp.7–16.

Gellner, E. (1992) *Reason and Culture. The Historic Role of Rationality and Rationalism*. Oxford: Blackwell.

Gibson, N. (1993) 'Images and Art – Interpretation and Meaning' in Starkings, D. (ed.) *Religion and the Arts in Education: Dimensions of Spirituality*. London: Hodder & Stoughton, pp.118–132.

Gilliat, P. (1996) 'Spiritual education and public policy 1944–1994' in Best, R. (ed.) *Education, Spirituality and the Whole Child*. London: Cassell, pp.161–172.

Giroux, H.A. (1994) *Disturbing Pleasures. Learning Popular Culture*. London: Routledge.

Green, J.L. (1985) 'The Concept of Reason in Hirst's Forms of Knowledge'. *Journal of Educational Thought*, 19:2, pp.109–116.

Green, R. (1993) 'Explorations in Music and Religion' in Starkings, D. (ed.) *Religion and the Arts in Education: Dimensions of Spirituality*. London: Hodder & Stoughton, pp.159–168.

Greenwood, B. (ed.) (1986) *Perspectives on Religious Education and Personal and Social Education*. London: CEM.

Griffiths, M. (1986) 'Hirst's Forms of Knowledge and Korner's Categorical Frameworks'. *Oxford Review of Education*, 12:1, pp.17–30.

Grimmitt, M. (1987) *Religious Education and Human Development. The Relationship Between Studying Religions and Personal, Social and Moral Education*. Great Wakering, Essex: McCrimmon.

Grove, J. (1993) 'Inspecting Spiritual and Moral Development'. *Resource*, 16:1, pp.13–14.

Gunton, C.E. (1985) *Enlightenment and Alienation. An Essay Towards a Trinitarian Theology*. Basingstoke: Marshall, Morgan & Scott.

Gunton, C.E. (1991) *The Promise of Trinitarian Theology*. Edinburgh: T. & T. Clark.

Gunton, C.E. (1993) *The One, the Three and the Many. God, Creation and the Culture of Modernity. The 1992 Bampton Lectures*. Cambridge: Cambridge University Press.

Habermas, J. (1987a) *Knowledge and Human Interests*. London: Polity Press.

Habermas, J. (1987b) *The Philosophical Discourse of Modernity*. London: Polity Press.

Habermas, J. (1987c) *The Theory of Communicative Action. Volume One. Reason and the Rationalisation of Society*. London: Polity Press.

Habermas, J. (1987d) *The Theory of Communicative Action. Volume Two. Lifeworld and System*. London: Polity Press.

Halstead, J.M. and Taylor, M.J. (eds) (1995) *Values in Education and Education in Values*. London: Falmer Press

Hammond, J. and Hay, D. (1992) '"When You Pray, Go To Your Private Room." A Reply to Adrian Thatcher'. *British Journal of Religious Education*, 14:3, pp.145–150.

Hammond, J., Hay, D., et al. (1990) *New Methods in RE Teaching*. Harlow: Oliver and Boyd.

Handelmann, S. (1982) *The Slayers of Moses. The emergence of Rabbinic interpretation in modern literary theory*. Albany: State University of New York Press.

Hardy, A. (1966) *The Divine Flame*. Oxford: Manchester College.

Hardy, A. (1979) *The Spiritual Nature of Man*. Oxford: Clarendon Press.

Harris, M. (1988) *Teaching and the Religious Imagination*. New York: Harper & Row.

Hart, C. (1994) *RE Changing the Agenda*. Newcastle-upon-Tyne: Christian Institute.

Hart, K. (1991) *The Trespass of the Sign. Deconstruction, Theology and Philosophy*. Cambridge: Cambridge University Press.

Hauerwas, S. (1995) *Dispatches From the Front: Theological Engagements with the Secular*. London: Duke University Press.

Hay, D. (1974) 'More Rumours of Angels'. *The Month*, 235, pp.796–799.

Hay, D. (1977) 'Religious Experience and Education'. *Learning For Living*. 16:4, pp.156–161.

Hay, D. (1982a) 'Teaching the Science of the Spirit' in Priestley, J.G. (ed.) *Religion, Spirituality and Schools. Perspectives 9*. Exeter: School of Education, University of Exeter, pp.37–53.

Hay, D. (1982b) *Exploring Inner Space. Is God still possible in the twentieth century?* Harmondsworth: Penguin Books.

Hay, D. (1985) 'Suspicion of the Spiritual: Teaching Religion in a World of Secular Experience'. *British Journal of Religious Education*, 7:3, pp.140–147, 134.

Hay, D. (1990) 'Religious Experience and Values' in Francis, L.J., Thatcher, A. (eds) *Christian Perspectives for Education*. Leominster: Gracewing / Fowler Wright, pp.350–354.

Hay, D. (1990) *Religious Experience Today: Studying the Facts*. London: Mowbray.

Hay, D., Nye, R. and Murphy, R. (1996) 'Thinking about childhood spirituality: review of research and current directions' in Francis, L.J., Kay, W.K., Campbell, W.S. (eds) *Research in Religious Education*. Leominster: Gracewing, pp.47–71.

Held, D. (1990) *Introduction to Critical Theory: Horkheimer to Habermas*. Cambridge: Polity Press.

Hick, J. (1977) *God and the Universe of Faiths*. London: Collins / Fount.

Hick, J. (1989) *An Interpretation of Religion. Human Responses to the Transcendent*. London: Macmillan.

Hick, J. and Knitter, P.F. (eds) (1987) *The Myth of Christian Uniqueness*. London: SCM.

Hill, B.V. (1989) '"Spiritual Development" in the Education Reform Act: A Source of Acrimony, Apathy or Accord?' *British Journal of Educational Studies*, 37:2, pp.169–182.

Hindess, E. (1972) 'Forms of Knowledge'. *Proceedings of the Philosophy of Education Society of Great Britain, Supplementary Issue*, 6:2, pp.164–175.

Hirst, P.H. (1965) 'Liberal Education and the Nature of Knowledge' in Archambault, R.D. (ed.) *Philosophical Analysis and Education*. London: Routledge & Kegan Paul, pp.113–138.

Hirst, P.H. (1972) 'The Nature of Educational Theory: Reply to D.J. O'Connor'. *Proceedings of the Philosophy of Education Society of Great Britain*, 6:1, pp.110–118.

Hirst, P.H. (1973) 'Forms of Knowledge: A reply to Elizabeth Hindess'. *Proceedings of the Philosophy of Education Society of Great Britain*, 7:2, pp.260–271.

Hirst, P.H. (1982) 'Philosophy of Education: The Significance of the Sixties'. *Educational Analysis*, 4:1, pp.5–10.

Hirst, P.H. and Peters, R.S. (1970) *The Logic of Education.* London: Routledge & Kegan Paul.

Holley, R. (1978) *Religious Education and Religious Understanding. An Introduction to the Philosophy of Religious Education.* London: Routledge & Kegan Paul.

Homan, R. (1995) 'Spiritual Education Across the Curriculum'. *SPES*, 2, pp.22–27.

Hudson, W.D. (1982) 'The Loneliness of the Religious Educator' in Priestley, J.G. (ed.) *Religion, Spirituality and Schools. Perspectives 9.* Exeter: School of Education, University of Exeter, pp.23–36.

Hull, J.M. (1989) *The Act Unpacked: the meaning of the 1988 Education Reform Act for religious education.* Derby: CEM.

Hull, J.M. (1992) 'Editorial: Religious Education and the Spiritual Rights of Children'. *British Journal of Religious Education*, 14:3, pp.129–131.

Hull, J.M. (1995a) 'Editorial: Collective Worship and the Search for the Spiritual'. *British Journal of Religious Education*, 17:2, pp.66–69.

Hull, J.M. (1995b) 'Editorial: Spiritual Education and the Money Culture'. *British Journal of Religious Education*, 17:3, pp.130–132.

Hull, J.M. (1995c) 'Collective Worship: The Search for Spirituality'. *Future Progress in Religious Education: The Templeton London Lectures at the RSA*, pp.27–38.

Hull, J.M. (1996) 'Editorial: God, Money and the Spirituality of Education'. *British Journal of Religious Education*, 18:2, pp.66–68.

Hulmes, E. (1979) *Commitment and Neutrality in RE.* London: Geoffrey Chapman.

Hulmes, E. (1982) 'The Education of Commitment' in Priestley, J.G. (ed.) *Religion, Spirituality and Schools. Perspectives 9.* Exeter: School of Education, University of Exeter, pp.54–66.

Hulmes, E. (1992) 'Unity and Diversity: The Search for Common Identity' in Watson, B. (ed.) *Priorities in Religious*

Education. A Model for the 1990s and Beyond. London: Falmer Press, pp.124–139.

Hume, D. (1947) *Dialogues Concerning Natural Religion*. Indianapolis: Bobbs-Merrill Educational.

Ingraffia, B.D. (1995) *Postmodern Theory and Biblical Theology: Vanquishing God's Shadow*. Cambridge: Cambridge University Press.

Islamic Academy (1993) *Spiritual and Moral Development: A Response to the NCC Discussion Paper*. Cambridge: Islamic Academy.

Jackson, R. (1993) 'Religious Education and the Arts of Interpretation' in Starkings, D. (ed.) *Religion and the Arts in Education: Dimensions of Spirituality*. London: Hodder & Stoughton, pp.148–158.

Jaki, S.L. (1978) *The Road of Science and the Ways of God. Gifford Lectures 1974–76*. Edinburgh: Scottish Academic Press.

James, W. (1960) *The Varieties of Religious Experience. A Study in Human Nature*. London: Fontana / Collins.

Jenkins, D. (1993) '"And She Supposing Him To Be The Gardener ..." Spirituality, the Arts and the Open Secret' in Starkings, D. (ed.) *Religion and the Arts in Education: Dimensions of Spirituality*. London: Hodder & Stoughton, pp.19–30.

Jungel, E. (1976) *The Doctrine of the Trinity. God's Being is in Becoming*. Edinburgh: Scottish Academic Press.

Jungel, E. (1983) *God as the Mystery of the World: On the Foundation of the Theology of the Crucified One in the Dispute between Theism and Atheism*. Edinburgh: T & T Clark.

Kafka, F. (1953) *The Trial*. Harmondsworth: Penguin Books.

Kafka, F. (1957) *The Castle*. Harmondsworth: Penguin Books.

Kant, I. (1934) *Critique of Pure Reason*. London: Dent

Kant, I. (1987) *Critique of Judgment*. Indianapolis: Hackett.

Kaufmann, W. (1974) *Nietzsche: Philosopher, Psychologist, Antichrist*. Princeton, New Jersey: Princeton University Press.

Kay, W.K. (1985) 'Variations on a Spiritual Theme: Man in a Multi-Faith World'. *British Journal of Religious Education*, 7:3, pp.128–134.

Kay, W.K. and Francis, L.J. (1996) *Drift from the Churches. Attitudes Toward Christianity During Childhood and Adolescence*. Cardiff: University of Wales Press.

Kelly, J.N.D. (1950) *Early Christian Creeds*. London: Longmans, Green & Co.

Kermode, F. (1971) *The Romantic Image*. London: Fontana.

Kerr, F. (1986) *Theology After Wittgenstein*. Oxford: Basil Blackwell.

Kibble, D.G. (1996) 'Spiritual development, spiritual experience and spiritual education' in Best, R. (ed.) *Education, Spirituality and the Whole Child*. London: Cassell, pp.64–74.

King, U. (1984a) *'RE: transcendence and liberation' Celebration and Challenge, full report on the conference at King's College to mark forty years of the 1944 Education Act, 13th June 1984*, London: CEM, pp.15–17.

King, U. (1984b) *Voices of Protest, Voices of Promise: Exploring Spirituality for a New Age. Hibbert Lecture 1984*. London: Hibbert Trust.

King, U. (1985) 'Spirituality in Secular Society: Recovering a Lost Dimension'. *British Journal of Religious Education*, 7:3, pp.135–139, 111.

King, U. (1993) *Women and Spirituality: Voices of Protest and Promise*. London: Macmillan Education.

King, U. (1995) 'The Complex Tapestry of Spirituality'. *Resource*, 17:3, pp.9–11.

Kirkland, J.P. (1996) 'Helping to restore spiritual values in abused children: a role for pastoral carers in education' in Best, R. (ed.) *Education, Spirituality and the Whole Child*. London: Cassell, pp.160–270.

Kung, H. (1980) *Does God Exist? An Answer for Today*. London: Collins.

Lambourn, D. (1996) '"Spiritual" minus "personal–social" =?: a critical note on an empty category' in Best, R. (ed.) *Education, Spirituality and the Whole Child*. London: Cassell, pp.150–158.

Lealman, B. (1982a) 'The Ignorant Eye: Perception and Religious Education'. *British Journal of Religious Education*, 4:2, pp.59–63.

Lealman, B. (1982b) 'Blue Wind and Broken Image' in Webster, D.H. and Tickner, M.F. (eds) *Religious Education and the Imagination. Aspects of Education: 28*. Hull: University of Hull Institute of Education, pp.74–84.

Lealman, B. (1986) 'Grottoes, Ghettos and City of Glass: Conversations about Spirituality'. *British Journal of Religious Education*, 8:2, pp.65–71.

Lealman, B. (1993) 'Drum, Whalebone and Dominant X: A Model for Creativity' in Starkings, D. (ed.) *Religion and the Arts in Education: Dimensions of Spirituality*. London: Hodder & Stoughton, pp.55–66

Lealman, B. (1996) 'The whole vision of the child' in Best, R. (ed.) *Education, Spirituality and the Whole Child*. London: Cassell, pp.20–29.

Lealman, B. and Robinson E. (1980) *The Image of Life*. London: CEM.

Lealman, B. and Robinson E. (1981) *Knowing and Unknowing*. London: CEM.

Lealman, B. and Robinson E. (1983) *The Mystery of Creation*. London: CEM.

Levi, P. (1979) *If This is a Man* and *The Truce*. Harmondsworth: Abacus, Sphere Books.

Levi, P. (1989) *The Drowned and the Saved*. Harmondsworth: Abacus, Sphere Books.

Liechty, D. (1990) *Theology in Postliberal Perspective*. London: SCM.

Lindbeck, G. A. (1984) *The Nature of Doctrine: Religion and Theology in a Postliberal Age.* London: SPCK.

Locke, J. (1968) *The Educational Writings of John Locke.* ed. Axtell, J.L. Cambridge: Cambridge University Press.

Locke, J. (1989) *Some Thoughts Concerning Education.* ed. John, W. and Yolton, J.S. Oxford: Clarendon Press.

Loukes, H. (1961) *Teenage Religion. An Enquiry into Attitudes and Possibilities Among British Boys and Girls in Secondary Modern Schools.* London: SCM.

Louth, A. (1989) *Discerning the Mystery. An Essay on the Nature of Theology.* Oxford: Clarendon Press.

Lyall, D. (1994) *Counselling in the Pastoral and Spiritual Context.* Buckingham: Open University Press.

Lyotard, J.-F. (1984) *The Postmodern Condition: A Report on Knowledge.* Manchester: Manchester University Press.

MacIntyre, A. (1985) *After Virtue. A Study in Moral Theory.* London: Duckworth.

MacIntyre, A. (1988) *Whose Justice? Whose Rationality?* London: Duckworth.

Mackley, J. (1993) *What is meant by spiritual development and how can the secondary school curriculum promote it? Farmington Fellowship.* Bristol: University of Bristol.

Maclure, J.S. (1968) *Educational Documents.* London: Methuen.

Macquarrie, J. (1972) *Paths in Spirituality.* London: SCM.

Mann, T. (1960) *The Magic Mountain.* Harmondsworth: Penguin Books.

Maxwell, N. (1987) *From Knowledge to Wisdom. A Revolution in the Aims and Methods of Science.* Oxford: Basil Blackwell.

McCreery, E. (1996) 'Talking to young children about things spiritual' in Best, R. (ed.) *Education, Spirituality and the Whole Child.* London.

McFadyen, A. I. (1990) *The Call To Personhood: A Christian Theory of the Individual in Social Relationships*. Cambridge: Cambridge University Press

McLaughlin, T.H. (1996) 'Education of the whole child?' in Best, R. (ed.) *Education, Spirituality and the Whole Child*. London: Cassell, pp.9–19.

Middleton, J.R. and Walsh, B.J. (1995) *Truth is Stranger Than it Used to Be: Biblical Faith in a Postmodern Age*. London. SPCK.

Milbank, J. (1993) *Theology and Social Theory: Beyond Secular Reason*. Oxford: Blackwell.

Miles, G. (1994) 'Transcendent and Religious Experiences of Sixth Form Pupils: An Analytic Model'. *SPES*, 1, pp.3–12.

Minney, R (1991) 'What is spirituality in an educational context?' *British Journal of Educational Studies*, 39:4, pp.386–397.

Minney, R. (1995) 'Are there Stages in Spiritual Development?' *SPES*, 2, pp.17–22.

Moltmann, J. (1974) *The Crucified God. The Cross of Christ as the Foundation and Criticism of Christian Theology*. London: SCM Press.

Mott-Thornton, K. (1996a) 'Language, Dualism and Experiential Religious Education: A critical appraisal of the debate between Adrian Thatcher and the authors of "New Methods in RE Teaching"'. *British Journal of Religious Education*, 18:3, pp.155–165.

Mott-Thornton, K. (1996b) 'Experience, critical realism and the schooling of spirituality' in Best, R. (ed.) *Education, Spirituality and the Whole Child*. London: Cassell, pp.75–92.

Muller, A. (1994) 'Cathedrals through the whole curriculum: a contribution to spirituality'. *British Journal of Religious Education*, 16:2.

Newbigin, L. (1986) *Foolishness to the Greeks. The Gospel and Western Culture*. London: SPCK.

Newby, M. (1994) 'The Spiritual Development of Children in a Secular Context: Reflections on some aspects of Theory and Practice'. *SPES,* 1, pp.17–20.

Newby, M. (1996) 'Towards a secular concept of spiritual maturity' in Best, R. (ed.) *Education, Spirituality and the Whole Child.* London: Cassell, pp.93–107.

Newman, J.H. (1919) *The Idea of a University.* London: Longman, Green & Co.

Nietzsche, F. (1986) *Human, All Too Human: A book for free spirits.* Cambridge: Cambridge University Press.

Norris, C. (1987) *Derrida.* London: Fontana.

Norris, C. (1993) *The Truth about Postmodernism.* Oxford: Blackwell.

Nye, R. (1996) 'Childhood spirituality and contemporary developmental psychology' in Best, R. (ed.) *Education, Spirituality and the Whole Child.* London: Cassell, pp.108–120.

Nye, R. and Hay, D. (1996) 'Identifying Children's Spirituality: How Do You Start Without a Starting Point?' *British Journal of Religious Education,* 18:3, pp.144–154.

O'Connor, D.J. (1972) 'The Nature of Educational Theory'. *Proceedings of the Philosophy of Education Society of Great Britain, Supplementary Issue,* 6:1, pp.97–109.

Ollington, J. (1982) 'Images for life' in Webster, D.H. and Tickner, M.F. (eds) *Religious Education and the Imagination. Aspects of Education: 28.* Hull: University of Hull Institute of Education, 63–73.

Paffard, M. (1973) *Inglorious Wordsworths.* London: Hodder & Stoughton.

Pannenberg, W. (1976) *Theology and the Philosophy of Science.* London: Darton, Longman and Todd.

Parker, D. (1995) 'OFSTED and the Provision in Schools for Children's Spiritual and Moral Development at Key Stages 1 and 2: Reflections'. *SPES,* 2, pp.5–6.

Pascal, B. (1966) *Pensées.* Harmondsworth: Penguin Books.

Paul, I. (1987) *Knowledge of God. Calvin, Einstein, and Polanyi.* Edinburgh: Scottish Academic Press.

Peacocke, A.R. (1971) *Science and the Christian Experiment.* Oxford: Oxford University Press.

Peacocke, A.R. (1984) *Intimations of Reality: Critical Realism in Science and Religion.* Indiana: University of Notre Dame Press.

Peacocke, A.R. (1993) *Theology for a Scientific Age.* London: SCM.

Peukert, H. (1986) *Science, Action and Fundamental Theology. Towards a Theology of Communicative Action.* Cambridge, Massachusetts: MIT Press.

Phenix, P. (1982) 'Promoting Personal Development Through Teaching' in Priestley, J.G. (ed.) *Religion, Spirituality and Schools. Perspectives 9.* Exeter: School of Education, University of Exeter.

Polanyi, M. (1958) *Personal Knowledge: Towards a Post-Critical Philosophy.* London: Routledge & Kegan Paul.

Polkinghorne, J. (1986) *One World: the interaction of science and theology.* London: SPCK.

Polkinghorne, J. (1988) *Science and Creation: the search for understanding.* London: SPCK.

Poole, M.W. (1995) *Beliefs and Values in Science Education.* Oxford: Oxford University Press.

Popper, K.R. (1966) *The Open Society and Its Enemies. Volume One: Plato.* London: Routledge & Kegan Paul.

Prentice, R. (1996) 'The spirit of education: a model for the twenty-first century' in Best, R. (ed.) *Education, Spirituality and the Whole Child.* London: Cassell, pp.319–342.

Priestley, J.G. (1982a) 'Teaching Transcendence' in Webster, D.H. and Tickner, M.F. (eds) *Religious Education and the Imagination. Aspects of Education: 28.* Hull: University of Hull Institute of Education.

Priestley, J.G. (1985) 'Towards Finding the Hidden Curriculum: A Consideration of the Spiritual Dimension of

Experience in Curriculum Planning'. *British Journal of Religious Education*, 7:3, pp.112–119.

Priestley, J.G. (1992) 'Whitehead Revisited – Religion and Education: An Organic Whole' in Watson, B. (ed.) *Priorities in Religious Education. A Model for the 1990s and Beyond.* London: Falmer Press.

Priestley, J.G. (ed.) (1982b) *Religion, Spirituality and Schools. Perspectives 9.* Exeter: School of Education, University of Exeter.

Reardon, B.M.G. (1985) *Religion in the Age of Romanticism. Studies in Early Nineteenth Century Thought.* Cambridge: Cambridge University Press.

Ricoeur, P. (1974) *The Conflict of Interpretations. Essays in Hermeneutics.* Evanston: Northwestern University Press.

Ricoeur, P. (1977) *The Rule of Metaphor. Multi-Disciplinary Studies in the Creation of Meaning in Language.* Toronto: University of Toronto Press.

Robinson, E. (1977a) *The Original Vision. A Study of the Religious Experience of Childhood.* Oxford: Manchester College.

Robinson, E. (1978) *Living the Questions. Studies in the Childhood of Religious Experience.* Oxford: Manchester College.

Robinson, E. (1982) 'Visual Aids and the Religious Imagination' in Webster, D.H. and Tickner, M.F. (eds) (1982) *Religious Education and the Imagination. Aspects of Education: 28.* Hull: University of Hull Institute of Education, pp.47–62.

Robinson, E. (1987) *The Language of Mystery.* London: SCM

Robinson, E. (ed.) (1977b) *This Time-Bound Ladder. Ten Dialogues on Religious Experience.* Oxford: Manchester College.

Rodger, A. (1996) 'Human spirituality: towards an educational rationale' in Best, R. (ed.) *Education, Spirituality and the Whole Child.* London: Cassell, pp.45–63.

Rorty, R. (1980) *Philosophy and the Mirror of Nature.* Oxford: Basil Blackwell.

Rorty, R. (1989) *Contingency, Irony and Solidarity.* Cambridge: Cambridge University Press.

Rose, D.W. (1996) 'Religious Education, Spirituality and the Acceptable Face of Indoctrination' in Best, R. (ed.) *Education, Spirituality and the Whole Child.* London: Cassell, pp.173–183.

Rossiter, M.C.G. (1996) 'The Secular Spirituality of Youth: Implications for Religious Education'. *British Journal of Religious Education*, 18:3, pp.133–143.

Rousseau, J.-J. (1986) *Emile.* London: Dent.

Rowe, D. (1996) 'Developing spiritual, moral and social values through a citizenship programme for primary schools' in Best, R. (ed.) *Education, Spirituality and the Whole Child.* London: Cassell, pp.285–293.

Rowling, L. (1996) 'Learning about life, teaching about loss' in Best, R. (ed.) *Education, Spirituality and the Whole Child.* London: Cassell, pp.271–284.

Rubenstein, R.L. (1966) *After Auschwitz. Radical Theology and Contemporary Judaism.* Indianapolis: Bobbs-Mevill.

Rubenstein, R.L. and Roth, J.K. (eds) (1987) *Approaches to Auschwitz: The Legacy of the Holocaust.* London: SCM.

Rudge, J. (1994) 'Religious Education and Spiritual Development'. *Resource*, 16:3, pp.2–6.

Sarup, M. (1988) *An Introductory Guide to Post-structuralism and Post-modernism.* London: Harvester Wheatsheaf.

Scarlett, B.F. (1984) 'Formal and Teleological Elements in Hirst's Argument for a Liberal Curriculum'. *Journal of Philosophy of Education*, 18:2, pp.155–165.

Schleiermacher, F.D.E. (1958) *On Religion: Speeches to its Cultured Despisers.* New York: Harper & Row.

Schleiermacher, F.D.E. (1976) *The Christian Faith.* Edinburgh: T. & T. Clark.

Shanks, A. (1995) *Civil Society, Civil Religion.* Oxford: Blackwell.

Simon, U.E. (1978a) *A Theology of Auschwitz.* London: SPCK.

Simon, U.E. (1978b) *Sitting in Judgement 1913–1963. An Interpretation of History.* London: SPCK.

Slee, N. (1992) '"Heaven in Ordinarie": The Imagination, Spirituality and the Arts in Religious Education' in Watson, B. (ed.) *Priorities in Religious Education. A Model for the 1990s and Beyond.* London: Falmer Press, pp.38–57.

Slee, N. (1993) 'Spirituality in education: an annotated bibliography'. *Journal of Beliefs and Values*, 13:2, pp.10–17.

Smart, N., Clayton, N., et al. (eds) (1985) *Nineteenth Century Religious Thought in the West. Volume One.* Cambridge: Cambridge University Press.

Smith, R.D. (1981) 'Hirst's Unruly Theory: forms of knowledge, truth and meaning'. *Educational Studies*, 7:1, pp.17–25.

Smith, W.C. (1978) *The Meaning and End of Religion: A New Approach to the Religious Traditions of Mankind.* London: SCM.

Sonneck, O.G. (ed.) (1954) *Beethoven: Impressions By His Contemporaries.* New York: Dover.

Souper, P. and Kay, W. (1982) *The School Assembly Debate: 1942–1982.* Southampton: University of Southampton Department of Education.

Souper, P.C. (ed.) (1985) *The Spiritual Dimension of Education. University of Southampton Department of Education, Occasional Paper No 2.* Southampton: University of Southampton.

Starkings, D. (1993b) 'The Landscape of Spirituality' in Starkings, D. (ed.) *Religion and the Arts in Education: Dimensions of Spirituality.* London: Hodder & Stoughton, pp.9–18.

Starkings, D. (ed.) (1993a) *Religion and the Arts in Education: Dimensions of Spirituality*. London: Hodder & Stoughton.

Stuart, B. (1996) 'Can the denominational sector offer a paradigm in RE?' in Best, R. (ed.) *Education, Spirituality and the Whole Child*. London: Cassell, pp.294–304.

Sutherland, S. (1995) 'The Spiritual and Moral Development of Children'. *Future Progress in Religious Education: The Templeton London Lectures at the RSA.*

Taylor, C. (1992) *Sources of the Self. The Making of the Modern Identity*. Cambridge: Cambridge University Press.

Taylor, M.C. (1982) *Deconstructing Theology*. New York: Crossroad Publishing.

Taylor, M.C. (1984) *Erring: A Postmodern A/theology*. Chicago: University of Chicago Press.

Thatcher, A. (1983) 'Learning to Become Persons: A Theological Approach to Educational Aims'. *Scottish Journal of Theology*, 36, pp.521–533.

Thatcher, A. (1991) 'A Critique of Inwardness in Religious Education'. *British Journal of Religious Education*, 14:1, pp.22–7.

Thatcher, A. (1993) 'Into Inwardsness Again ...'. *British Journal of Religious Education*, 15:3, pp.53–54.

Thatcher, A. (1996) '"Policing the Sublime": a wholly (holy?) ironic approach to the spiritual development of children' in Astley, J., Francis, L.J. (eds) *Christian Theology and Religious Education: Connections and Contradictions*. London: SPCK, pp.117–139.

Thomas, T. (ed.) (1988) *The British: Their Religious Beliefs and Practices*. London: Routledge.

Thompson, R. (1990) *Holy Ground. The Spirituality of Matter*. London: SPCK.

Tillich, P. (1963) *Christianity and the Encounter of World Religions*. Columbia: Columbia University Press.

Torrance, T.F. (1962) *Karl Barth. An Introduction to his Early Theology 1910–1931.* London: SCM.

Torrance, T.F. (1965) *Theology in Reconstruction.* London: SCM.

Torrance, T.F.(1969) *Theological Science.* Oxford: Oxford University Press.

Torrance, T.F.(1980) *The Ground and Grammar of Theology.* Belfast: Christian Journals.

Tracey, D. (1981) *The Analogical Imagination. Christian Theology and the Culture of Pluralism.* London: SCM.

Trainor, D. (1995) 'The Inspection of Spiritual and Moral Development'. *SPES*, 2, pp.3–4.

Ungoed-Thomas, J. (1996) 'Respect for persons: a curricular crisis of identities' in Best, R. (ed.) *Education, Spirituality and the Whole Child.* London: Cassell, pp.121–138.

Ungoed-Thomas, J.R. (1986) 'Personal and Social Education and Spiritual Development' in Greenwood, B. (ed.) *Perspectives on Religious Education and Personal and Social Education.* London: CEM.

Ungoed-Thomas, J.R. (1990) 'Personal and social education, religious education and spiritual development' in Francis, L. and Thatcher, A. (eds) *Christian Perspectives for Education.* Leominster: Gracewing / Fowler Wright, pp.340–349.

Usher, R. and Edwards, R. (1994) *Postmodernism and Education.* London: Routledge.

Wach, J. (1958) *The Comparative Study of Religion.* New York: Columbia University Press.

Wach, J. (1962) *Sociology of Religion.* Chicago: University of Chicago Press.

Wakefield, G.S. (ed.) (1983) *A Dictionary of Christian Spirituality.* London: SCM.

Wall, B. (1993) 'Rhyme and Reason: Religious Education through the Arts' in Starkings, D. (ed.) *Religion and the Arts in Education: Dimensions of Spirituality.* London: Hodder & Stoughton, pp.179–188.

Walsh, W.H. (1967) 'Kant, Immanuel' in Edwards, P. (ed.) (1967) *The Encyclopedia of Philosophy. Volume Three.* London: Collier-Macmillan, pp.305–324.

Warner, M. (1996) 'Headteachers' perceptions of their role in spiritual education: some empirical data and a discussion' in Best, R. (ed.) *Education, Spirituality and the Whole Child.* London: Cassell, pp.222–242.

Watson, B. (1993a) *The Effective Teaching of Religious Education.* London: Longman.

Watson, B. (1993b) 'The Arts as a Dimension of Religion' in Starkings, D. (ed.) *Religion and the Arts in Education: Dimensions of Spirituality.* London: Hodder & Stoughton, pp.95–105.

Watson, B. (ed.) (1992) *Priorities in Religious Education. A Model for the 1990s and Beyond.* London: Falmer Press.

Webster, D.H. (1982a) 'Awe in the Curriculum' in Priestley, J.G. (ed.) *Religion, Spirituality and Schools. Perspectives 9.* Exeter: School of Education, University of Exeter, pp.67–84.

Webster, D.H. (1982b) 'Spiritual Growth in Religious Education' in Webster, D.H. and Tickner. M.F. (eds) *Religious Education and the Imagination. Aspects of Education: 28.* Hull: University of Hull Institute of Education, pp.85–95.

Webster, D.H. (1985) 'Commitment, Spirituality and the Classroom'. *British Journal of Religious Education,* 8:1, pp.20–25, 29.

Webster, D.H. (1990) 'A Spiritual Dimension for Education?' in Francis, L.J. and Thatcher, A. (eds) *Christian Perspectives for Education.* Leominster: Gracewing / Fowler Wright, pp.356–364.

Webster, D.H. (1993) 'Being Aflame: Spirituality in County and Church Schools' in Francis, L.J. and Lankshear, D.W. (eds) *Christian Perspectives on Church Schools: A Reader.* Leominster, Herefordshire: Gracewing / Fowler Wright, pp.130–140.

Webster, D.H. (1996) 'Spiders and eternity: spirituality and the curriculum' in Best, R. (ed.) *Education, Spirituality and the Whole Child*. London: Cassell, pp.245–259.

Webster, D.H. and Tickner, M.F. (eds) (1982) *Religious Education and the Imagination. Aspects of Education: 28*. Hull: University of Hull Institute of Education.

White, J. (1994) 'Instead of OFSTED: a critical discussion of OFSTED on spiritual, moral, social and cultural development'. *Cambridge Journal of Education*, 24:3, pp.369–377.

White, J. (1996) 'Education, spirituality and the whole child: a humanist perspective' in Best, R. (ed.) *Education, Spirituality and the Whole Child*. London: Cassell, pp.30–42.

Whitehead, A.N. (1970) *The Aims of Education and Other Essays*. New York: Macmillan Free Press.

Wiggershaus, R. (1995) *The Frankfurt School. Its History, Theories and Political Significance*. Cambridge: Polity Press.

Wilson, J. (1971) *Education in Religion and the Emotions*. London: Heinemann.

Wright, A. (1993) *Religious Education in the Secondary School: Prospects for Religious Literacy*. London: David Fulton.

Wright, A. (1995) 'The Integrity and Provenance of Religious Education. Modernism, Deconstruction and Critical Realism'. Unpublished PhD thesis, University of London.

Wright, A. (1996a) 'Language and Experience in the Hermeneutics of Religious Understanding'. *British Journal of Religious Education*, 18:3, pp.166–180.

Wright, A. (1996b) 'The Child in Relationship: Towards a Communal Model of Spirituality' in Best, R. (ed.) *Education, Spirituality and the Whole Child*. London: Cassell, pp.139–149.

Wright, A. (1996c) 'Postmodernism and Religious Education: A Reply to Liam Gearon'. *Journal of Beliefs and Values*, 17:1, pp.19–25.

Yeomans, R. (1993a) 'Religious Art and Spiritual Art: Spiritual Values and Early Modernist Painting' in Starkings, D. (ed.) *Religion and the Arts in Education: Dimensions of Spirituality.* London: Hodder & Stoughton, pp.70–82.

Yeomans, R. (1993b) 'Islam: The Abstract Expression of Spiritual Values' in Starkings, D. (ed.) *Religion and the Arts in Education: Dimensions of Spirituality.* London: Hodder & Stoughton, pp.83–94.

Yu, C.T. (1987) *Being and Relation. A Theological Critique of Western Dualism and Individualism.* Edinburgh: Scottish Academic Press.